The Entrenchment of the 'unus alterum' Pattern

ŁÓDŹ
STUDIES IN LANGUAGE
Edited by
Barbara Lewandowska-Tomaszczyk
and Łukasz Bogucki

Vol. 49

PETER LANG
EDITION

Mikołaj Nkollo

The Entrenchment
of the 'unus alterum' Pattern

Four Essays on Latin and
Old Romance Reciprocal Constructions

PETER LANG
EDITION

Bibliographic Information published by the Deutsche Nationalbibliothek
The Deutsche Nationalbibliothek lists this publication in the Deutsche
Nationalbibliografie; detailed bibliographic data is available in the internet at
http://dnb.d-nb.de.

Library of Congress Cataloging-in-Publication Data
Names: Nkollo, Mikołaj, author.
Title: The entrenchment of the 'unus alterum' pattern / Mikołaj Nkollo.
Description: Frankfurt am Main ; New York : Peter Lang, 2016. | Series:
Łódź studies in language | Includes bibliographical references and index.
Identifiers: LCCN 2016030211 | ISBN 9783631676592
Subjects: LCSH: Romance languages--Reciprocals. | Grammar, Comparative and
general--Reciprocals.
Classification: LCC PC61 .N56 2016 | DDC 440/.045--dc23 LC record available at
https://lccn.loc.gov/2016030211

The book is part of the research project funded by the
National Centre of Science (decision: DEC-2012/07/B/HS2/00602).

NATIONAL SCIENCE CENTRE
POLAND

This publication has been peer-reviewed in a double-blind process.

ISSN 1437-5281
ISBN 978-3-631-67659-2 (Print)
E-ISBN 978-3-653-07067-5 (E-PDF)
E-ISBN 978-3-631-69437-4 (EPUB)
E-ISBN 978-3-631-69438-1 (MOBI)
DOI 10.3726/978-3-653-07067-5

© Peter Lang GmbH
Internationaler Verlag der Wissenschaften
Frankfurt am Main 2016
All rights reserved.
Peter Lang Edition is an Imprint of Peter Lang GmbH.

Peter Lang – Frankfurt am Main · Bern · Bruxelles · New York ·
Oxford · Warszawa · Wien

This publication has been peer reviewed.

www.peterlang.com

Table of contents

Introduction

1.1 Aims and scope. Diachronic shifts in the marking of reciprocity

The aims pursued in the present monograph relate to the emergence and further development of reciprocal constructions with the sequence descending from *unus alterum* in Old Romance languages. The fortunes of this expression, prior to the rise of medieval neo-Latin vernaculars, is quite intriguing. As a matter of fact, in spite of being abundantly documented in late Latin texts, *unus alterum* seems to have been rather peripheral in previous periods of the history of the Latin language. Compared to the multitude of specialized bipartite markers (i.e. those that cannot be used interchangeably), the number of its attestations in classical writings is fairly small. Yet, right from the outset of the Romance era, instead of relying on semantically well-defined reiterated expressions (see 1a-b below), reciprocity is nearly universally encoded by linguistic signs originating from *unus alterum* and by the former reflexive pronoun < *se* (acc./abl.). Thus, an ancillary concern, which helps shed light on properly Romance matters, is the reconstruction of how this quantitative impoverishment actually came about. Latin data, extensively dealt with in Essay 1, is expected to explain why an erstwhile marginal expression went ahead of its rivals, reputedly more widespread.

(1a) *Omnium namque malorum in Sergio Verginioque causas esse; nec id accusatorem magis arguere quam fateri reos, qui noxii ambo **alter in alterum** causam conferant, fugam Sergi Verginius, Sergius proditionem increpans Vergini* Livy *UC* 5, 11 (TLL) 'For that the sources of all their sufferings were centred in Sergius and Virginius: nor did the prosecutor advance that charge more satisfactorily than the accused acknowledged it; who, both guilty, threw the blame from one to the other, Virginius charging Sergius with running away, Sergius charging Virginius with treachery' (transl. PG)

(1b) *Quam ob rem, si hoc iudici praescriptum lege aut officio putatis, testibus credere, nihil est cur **alius alio** iudice melior aut sapientior existimetur* Cic. *Font* 22 (LC) 'If therefore you think that a juryman has either a legal or a moral obligation to believe witnesses, then there can be no reason for judging one juryman to be better or wiser than another' (transl. LC)

Eventually, no semantic loss in the functional domain of reciprocity is revealed in Old Romance languages. Although they exploit a single bipartite marker, the same range of meanings as in Latin is successfully transmitted. Thus, Romance reciprocal sequences originating from *unus alterum* prove astonishingly resilient and efficient in accommodating all semantic varieties that were formally distinct in classical Latin. This meaning-preserving uniformity poses an additional challenge: the study is expected to account for how the loss of numerous formal variants was made up for.

More properly explanatory issues are addressed in the analyses of language-specific grammatical phenomena. In each of these parts, detailed semantic and grammatical problems are approached. Their strongly individuated nature is better grasped if constructions drawn from two Old Romance languages are set off against each other. In spite of the fact that they denote similar types of relation (hitting; see 2a–b below), the two sentences are substantially different in how their markers are linearly arranged. Moreover, inflectional characteristics of the verbal predicate in French 12th-century example stand in a stark contrast to the Spanish (14th century) singular *plaga* 'wounds'. If the hypothesis according to which two non–synonymous meanings tend to be mirrored by divergent syntactic structures is agreed on, even these sketchy illustrations show how pervasive the differences between language-specific constructions are.

> (2a) *Todo hombre que* **plaga uno a otro** *& si el plagado se clamare alos mayorales de conceyllo. los mayorales deuen fer luego coyllir fiança del fuero al clamant*, Fuero de la Novenera, fol. 1r (HSMS) 'Each time that two men injure each other, if the wounded brings a claim to the mayors of the council, the mayors are obliged to provide him with a confirmation pursuant the Fuero'
> (2b) *Et* **fierent** *de si grant vertu* **li uns l'autre** *sor son escu*, Cligès, v.3551–3552 (DÉCT) 'They hit each other's shield vigorously'

As all these individual cases cannot be easily interconnected (besides dealing with reciprocal constructions, hardly any common points are found), the structure of the book has been deliberately planned as disparate. Rather than a continuous and consistent portrayal of Old Romance reciprocity, the readers are being offered a series of essays, focusing on reciprocal sequences in Old French, Old Spanish and Old Portuguese. Yet, the matters dwelt upon in this book are believed to be of more than ordinary theoretical import for the functional domain of reciprocity and the evolution of units serving to encode it. Thus, detailed aims to be achieved are listed below.

Essay 3, devoted to Old French, addresses the following problems: Except for their frequency in medieval texts, how are reciprocal constructions with *l'un l'autre* different from their Latin forerunners? What kind of evolutionary mechanisms, collective or individually performed, are implicated in their further formal processing? How do these mechanisms defy pre-existent opinions about the origin of grammatical shifts? Do the newly created models become paired with new semantic variants of reciprocity?

The concept of the diachronic layer is pivotal in essay 4. The analysis focuses on why some of the Latin reiterated clusters continued to coexist and interact with the *uno a otro* marker. The persistence of archaic reciprocal constructions informs our knowledge of layering insofar as it highlights syntactic and semantic environments likely to privilege old structures at the expense of the newer ones. Finally, an important aspect of the essay revolves around the cross-linguistic significance of morphological facts detectable in Old Spanish reciprocal sequences. Thus, their analysis can refine our understanding of some concepts recurrently debated in typological linguistics.

The last essay is primarily concerned with the consequences of the semantic closeness between various kinds of reciprocal constructions. The analysis of 15th-century texts by one author helps ascertain whether close meaning interrelationships always entail the increase in the syntactic homogeneity of a given class of constructions. Additionally, data retrieved from Fernão Lopes's chronicles reshapes our understanding of the role of individually performed innovations. Finally, the discussion will touch upon whether the entrenchment of new form-meaning pairs comes about in a more abrupt or a more gradual manner.

Detailed aims, as singled out in the preceding paragraphs, reveal the general lines of interest of the present study. The overarching process to be investigated in all the four essays is grammatical evolution. Many findings in this field achieved thus far by grammaticalization theory are obvious and are not going to be called into question in the present monograph. Yet, the very concept of grammaticalization defined, in keeping with Kuryłowicz's (1975[1965]: 52) seminal insights, as the drift of the former lexical items towards grammatical ones (see also 'Reduced to its essentials, grammaticalization theory begins with the observation that grammatical morphemes develop gradually out of lexical morphemes or combinations of lexical morphemes with lexical or grammatical morphemes', Bybee, Perkins & Pagliuca 1994: 4), will be applied only sparingly. Special caution is needed with most radical assumptions of this theoretical stance. Some of them have never received sufficient empirical confirmation. One of the cogent illustrations is the claim that all grammatical markers can be ultimately traced back to content words, either directly or through the intermediary of other grammatical markers that once used to be straightforwardly lexical[1] (see Diessel, 2006: 474,

---

1 The concept of secondary grammaticalization has been coined to circumvent this problem and to account for instances of evolution in which a grammatical item drifts towards an even greater degree of grammaticality. An exemplary representation of the difference between the two types is: 1. lexical verb > 2. auxiliary > 3. clitic auxiliary > 4. inflectional ending. The process tying the stages 1 and 2 is an instance of primary

commenting on an earlier version of Hopper and Traugott, 2003). The thing is that grammatical items originating from putatively lexical sources frequently fail to be convincingly reconstructed.

Moreover, some of the properties of Old Romance reciprocal constructions are not amenable to judgements couched in terms of 'more grammatical' or 'less grammatical'. For example, no method has been devised to decide which kind of morphological exponents, cumulative or split, has a more grammatical status. Yet, this issue has a direct bearing on how reciprocity used to be encoded in classical Latin and in Old Romance. In Latin sequences such as *Manus manum lavat* 'one hand washes the other', the expression of reciprocity alongside temporal information and the quantificational force of NPs is taken care of by a single sign: the juxtaposition of two inflectional forms of a single common noun. By contrast, in Romance languages these pieces of information are split, i.e. distributed over various elements of the sentence. Hardly could these differences be characterized as representing the drift from lexicon to grammar, or the other way round. Even if a more up-to-date definition is evoked, conceiving of grammaticalization as 'a process in which it [i.e. a linguistic sign] loses in autonomy by becoming more subject to constraints of the linguistic system' (Lehmann, 2004: 155), medieval reciprocal markers should be re-examined to ascertain whether they had been less autonomous and more constrained than their Latin forerunners. Possibly, then, their evolution cannot be equated with grammaticalization pure and simple, thus calling for an alternative explanation.

---

grammaticalization. The remaining shifts are secondary. Thus, primary grammaticalization (lexical > grammatical) is a prerequisite for instances of secondary grammaticalization (less grammatical > more grammatical). Another case in point is the origin of Romance reciprocal markers and constructions. Out of five developmental paths that lead cross-linguistically to grammatical exponents of reciprocity (Heine & Miyashita, 2008: 176–186; Maslova & Nedjalkov, 2013), only one has a clear-cut lexical starting point: nouns denoting symmetric relations (e.g. *friend, mate, neighbour*; see below) have been demonstrated to give rise to reciprocal markers in some languages. The remaining sources either look more like highly routinized templates enabling speakers to bring the names of participants and the name of the relation together (repetition > reciprocal marker, contrast > reciprocal marker), or are already earmarked for conveying meanings associated with other categories (collective > reciprocal marker, reflexive > reciprocal marker). Old Romance reciprocal markers are known to have originated mainly from the Latin reflexive and from *unus alterum*. By contrast, purely lexical items played merely a marginal role (Nkollo, 2013b: 290–293). Thus, the already constrained and schematic status of this class of linguistic signs poses a serious challenge to the assumptions of grammaticalization theory.

Instead of using the conceptual apparatus of grammaticalization theory in an indiscriminate way, the present study relies on a more moderate concept of re-grammation. It has been coined to circumscribe any instances of reorganization within a given grammatical system (Lindschouw, 2010: 182). Its usefulness is due to the fact that, compared to their common Latin ancestor, in various areas of their grammars, Romance languages are considered to represent various degrees of innovativeness. Obviously, all the deviations from classical patterns are not of equal depth. Whereas some of them proceeded via a series of erosive shifts (in keeping with what grammaticalization theory predicts), others exhibit a less radical character.

1.2 Key theoretical assumptions

1.2.1 Construction grammar

Although this monograph consists of a series of case studies, some common background has been looked for to deal with particular problems in a princi-pled and consistent manner. An absolute methodological homogeneity has not been achieved. In the essays that follow, some of the assumptions stemming from Government and Binding and from competing motivations frameworks are going to be exploited in a subsidiary way. Yet, it is Construction Grammar (henceforth CxG) that lays down most general guidelines for the present study. For scholars who subscribe to its tenets, the basic unit of analysis is unanimously equated with conventional linkages between a particular form and a particular meaning or discourse function. In the growing body of work representing this epistemological stance, grammar is conceived of as a hierarchized set of con-structions, i.e. a repository of such 'form-meaning pairs'. It encompasses both individually specified expressions, including idiomatic ones and highly produc-tive abstract schemas, constantly recurrent in a given language. Generalizations about speakers' linguistic knowledge are captured by identifying clusters of co-occurring features (see footnote 2).

Before going on to a more in-depth presentation of CxG, it should be borne in mind that constructions must not be confused with constructs. The former are higher-level, abstract 'pieces of grammar' (Kay & Fillmore 1999: 2), whereas con-structs correspond to physical realizations of constructions and are materialized in authentic utterances. In other words, constructions surface in actual discourse events as constructs. This distinction gains importance as soon as the role of con-structions in diachronic processes is to be clarified: partial transitions and small scale changes that an expression is subject to can cumulate and ultimately prompt the emergence of a new form-meaning pair, or modify radically an already existing one. Yet, the locus for the change resides invariably in constructs, but obviously not in constructions. The significance of this distinction will be revealed in the essay dealing with individually performed innovations in Old Portuguese.

The context in which linguistic and discourse units are located is another aspect of vital importance to constructionist analyses. Every instance of change is always triggered in a particular local setting, i.e. a confluence of semantic, pragmatic and syntactic factors. Thus, not only do constructions represent the endpoint of an evolution, they can also be thought of as the domain of change. If the number of their attestations is sufficient, concrete constructs (C1, C2, C3...Cn) of a certain shape, eventually contribute to the emergence of a construction X. The process is often facilitated by another, independent but in some respects similar, construction Y. In other words, a particular combination of units in an utterance may become a unit on its own. As a side-effect, the new form-meaning pair acquires a non-predictable meaning or discourse function. Therefore, with regard to the domain of change, constructions are both the source of analogical motivations and the outcome of syntactic reanalysis.

The development of CxG was spurred, among other things, after scholars had realized that speakers' implicit language skills did not boil down to the mere recognition of the meaning of individual linguistic signs and separate expressions. Instead, language processing involves knowledge of the ways in which signs of various sizes are used in actual communication. Therefore, in CxG no distinction between linguistic form and its meaning, discourse function, and principles of usage is made. All these dimensions are brought together to form constructions, i.e. conventional patterns of speakers' understanding.

If the global linguistic and discursive status of constructions cannot be predicted felicitously by simply adding the meanings of their constituents[2], scholars

---

2   An integrated, anti-modular, treatment of constructions does not mean that scholars cannot take 'a glimpse inside' to see how they are configured (Fried, 2013: 428). Form-meaning pairs are frequently represented as bundles of features. An essential aspect of such representations consists in tracing a dividing line between 'external' and 'internal' (or constituent-level) properties. The former identify a construction as a whole, by exposing its conventional characteristics. They account for how a given expression is constrained and how it can interact with other patterns. By contrast, internal properties focus on individual features of a construction's constituents. Thus, not only do systematic generalizations about how a given construction fits in with larger grammatical structures become available, but a picture of the internal make-up of constructions is offered accordingly.

are led into accepting that their semantic or discourse values must be associated with the pattern as a whole. The significance of this point extends once more over how constructions evolve. Diachronically, non-compositionality is capable of accounting for how transitions between various stages come about: evolutions lead from a (more) compositional to a non-compositional pattern. This is to say that over the course of time, language develops because its users strive to meet two concomitant needs: the need to coin an increasing number of new expressions with fully transparent meanings and the need to reanalyse extant combinations, providing them with new semantic values. The latter process nearly always entails the loss of semantic transparency.

Moreover, constructional opacity implies that some lexical items are themselves constructions. For instance, since in no way can the meaning 'to fall asleep' be associated with the French sequence [sãdɔʀmiʀ], the problem can be overcome only if one accepts that *s'endormir* itself is a conventional association of a given phonetic shape and a given meaning (Waltereit, 2012: 6–7). Therefore, the grammar at each stage of its history can be thought of as a fluctuating network of interwoven patterns with various degrees of intricacy and generality. In this way, CxG provides a tool for capturing the underlying principles of grammar and lexicon in a holistic way and circumscribes speakers' implicit knowledge of particular language facts. Rather than bringing together forms one by one to eventually derive a global meaning, speakers tend to rely on larger patterns. Instead of being processed on the basis of the individual properties of their parts, constructions are stored in memory as such and can be readily accessed each time they are needed in an utterance (Gras, 2011: 167–168). A natural consequence of this assumption is that lexicon and grammar are not separate components of a linguistic system. Instead of having their parts distributed over independent modules, they are more adequately approached as overlapping levels of analysis sharing the same nature.

Yet, the lexical *vs.* grammatical dichotomy has not been done away with altogether in the constructionist approach. The difference between them lies in the fact that they are placed at various points along the directional cline extending from the substantive to the schematic pole (Gisborne & Patten, 2011: 96–98)[3].

---

3 Being schematic implies not having phonological substance. Conversely, being substantive requires an item to surface as phonetically specified material. The semantic feature [+ introduces what is going to be said or done] found in the procedural *Let me give you an example* or *Let me just finish this and then I'll come* (Traugott & Dasher, 2005: 176–177) has no phonological substance on its own. This feature manifests itself with no tangible sound material. In this respect it differs radically from the way the sound substance in *s'endormir* identifies this item. The formal side of *let somebody /*

Whereas grammatical structures are usually highly schematic and recurrent, form-meaning correspondences traditionally assumed to belong to lexicon have a more individuated and substantive nature (Waltereit, 2012: 6–7). In order for a given form-meaning pair to reach the status of a full-fledged construction, schemata and substances are in a constant interplay. 'More lexical' and 'more grammatical' are overlaid by another distinction: atomic vs. complex. Atomic constructions are not made of many elements, i.e. are syntactically simple. Accordingly, complex constructions necessarily involve more than one meaningful part (Croft, 2001: 14–17). Simplifying somewhat, the following diagram accounts for how constructional dimensions happen to be cross-cut.

FIG. 1 *Constructional dimensions (based on Trousdale, 2012: 172)*

	Substantive	Schematic
Atomic	*dire*	Verb
Complex	*vient de dire*	Passé récent

As it is identified with the sound material [diʀ], the infinitive *dire* can be seemingly classified as substantive and atomic. Yet, on closer inspection, its straightforwardly substantive status does not go unchallenged. The item is schematic in that it predetermines a series of slots for its arguments. The latter are coerced into filling fixed positions. In spite of the multitude of possible realizations of some of its arguments, all of them are substantive constructions superimposed onto an abstract linear template. By contrast, Verb is a highly schematic category, whose most prominent, albeit not exclusive, task is to encode concepts pivotal to the propositional content of the sentence. Unlike verbal lexemes found in actual utterances, no phonetic substance corresponds to this category in Romance languages. At the same time, Verb is an atomic entity, hence unlikely to be split into constructions of smaller size. French form-meaning pair known as passé recent (for its comprehensive analysis; see Bres & Labeau, 2015: 537–548) is both schematic and complex, whereas one of its textual manifestations *Il vient de dire* is complex and surfaces as a substantive sequence. Regardless of the fact that the above mentioned constructions have divergent characteristics, all of them are meaningful linguistic units[4].

---

something do something is reduced to providing slots for a proposition and a pronoun syntactically subordinate to *let*. Nevertheless, this schema is obviously meaningful in much the same way as a substantive item *s'endormir* is.

4   Schematic constructions tend to be intuitively associated with complexity, whereas substantive form-meaning pairs are usually seen as being close to the atomic pole. Yet,

1.2.2 Grammaticalization of constructions

A natural corollary of having chosen construction grammar as a methodological background underlying the foregoing analyses is the need to find out how constructions grammaticalize. This brings us back to grammaticalization theory. In what follows, it is hypothesized that the way constructions evolve is best grasped by some of the conceptual tools worked out by the representatives of grammaticalization theory. In spite of the scepticism towards some of its claims, certain research agendas are apparently common to both frameworks. Each of them is well suited to the goal of representing the predominant influence of context on the development of new discourse units and grammatical patterns. Thus, the two approaches concur in highlighting the close connection between linguistic change and language use. Finally, the need to capture the essentially dynamic nature of language units' life cycle, as well as the gradualness of grammatical change are brought to the fore in each of them.

The intersection of the two perspectives is immediately perceived as soon as the syntagmatic behaviour of language units in evolutionary processes is considered. Research on grammaticalization arose with the interest in the role of collocations (Fried, 2013: 420). This idea has been expressly articulated by Lehmann (1995[1982]: 406) who states: 'grammaticalization does not merely seize a word or morpheme [...] but the whole construction formed by the syntagmatic relations of the element in question'. Thus, the principles of language use are neatly accommodated within the study of meaning shifts that accompany grammaticalization.

To give but one rather uncomplicated example of how contextual factors are present in language changes, the French *ÊTRE en train de* V_{inf} 'to be in the process of (doing)' construction is going to be briefly reminded. Apparently, it is

---

some classes of language units systematically contradict these preconceived ideas. On the one hand, idiomatic expressions, like Portuguese *bater as botas* 'kick the bucket', *estar com dor de cotovelo* 'to be jealous', etc. are, at the same time, complex and substantive. On the other, parts of speech are predominantly indivisible, yet schematic. For example, since French adjectives may ordinarily co-occur with intensifiers or be subject to gradation (in which case many of them must have their arguments) or agree in number and gender with their head noun, they share a set of abstract, linguistically relevant characteristics. Importantly, these features encompass both the whole class and its individual members. Moreover, the category itself surfaces with no recurrent sound material, thus gaining an undisputedly schematic status. By contrast, to be communicatively viable, the category needs to be overlaid by particular expressions, such as *jaune* 'yellow', *coupable* 'guilty', *acerbe* 'bitter, acerbic'. Thus, what is being dealt with here are substances superimposed onto schemes.

located somewhere in the middle of the substantive–schematic cline: on the one hand, some of its items are fixed in advance (the presence of one of the inflectional variants of *ÊTRE*, the noun *train*, the initially locative *en* preposition, and the complementizer *de* are not subject to substitution; *en train de* is a complex, linearly constrained string). On the other, the construction leaves room for variable units, as well: the person / number / tense / mood of *ÊTRE* and the infinitive, which are atoms in particular constructs ('micro-constructions' in Traugott's terminology; cf. Traugott, 2008: 32), can vary. Thus, it is not enough to conclude that an erstwhile locative / existential verb *ÊTRE* has gradually acquired an even more abstract grammatical function (its role is to contribute to marking 'l'aspect duratif de l'action, le procès en voie de s'accomplir ou l'évolution d'un état'; TLFi, www.cnrtl.fr/definition/train). Rather, this specific value developed in a particular structural environment[5]. The simplistic idea that the whole construction changes its status over time is of no interest.

By contrast, what is being dealt with here is the interaction of various subsets of features that co-occur in actual constructs and that give rise to a new pattern with a non-transparent meaning. In diachronic analyses, the distinction between 'internal' and 'external' properties of constructions (see footnote 2 above) proves very helpful: grammaticalization proceeds through the readjustment of features. The accumulation of such small scale shifts leads to a perceptible change of the shape of a given sequence, possibly involving a new syntactic node (Trousdale, 2014: 564). As a result, the grammatical status of the pattern is completely different from what it used to be in the previous occurrences of its parts. Both construction grammar and grammaticalization theory are particularly interested in capturing the incremental character of the change and in accounting for possible mismatches between larger grammar patterns and individual values of the items composing them.

Aside from the role of context in diachronic processes, at least the following interrelated points attract the attention of the adherents of the two frameworks: the gradualness of change and intermediate stages likely to prefigure upcoming directions of an evolutionary cline; polysemy and layering phenomena as indicative

---

5   Much in the same vein, Heine and Kuteva (2005: 15) propose four parameters to describe the grammaticalization of forms and constructions: a) extension, i.e. the rise of novel grammatical meanings when linguistic expressions are extended to new contexts (context-induced reinterpretation); b) desemanticization, i.e. loss or generalization of meaning; c) decategorialization, i.e. decrease in morphosyntactic properties typically characterising lexical or other less grammaticalized forms, and d) phonetic reduction, i.e. loss of phonetic substance, including cliticization.

of partial transitions between various synchronically circumscribed stages; and, finally, the role of analogical extensions in the emergence of new constructions.

All in all, grammaticalization of constructions reaches its peak only at the stage when the new meaning of an item is inextricably linked with a particular sequence of elements and / or particular slots within this sequence. It is frequently the case that an original configuration with a new syntactic node emerges in such cases. To revert to the discussion about the lexeme *DIRE*, a series of innovative uses of some of its inflectional variants can easily be spotted in present-day French. For example, its conditional forms seem to be particularly well-suited to convey the idea of approximation or rough-and-ready comparison (*dirais-je, comme qui dirait, dirait-on*, etc.). Yet, they do so only after certain structural requirements are met (e.g. inverted subject-verb order, parenthetical position). This is an instance of directional change, in which an erstwhile atomic element, for it is obligatorily accompanied by other units, becomes part of a more complex assemblage. Likewise, these novel uses are indicative of the increasingly schematic status of the forms of *DIRE*. No sound substance can be directly associated with the idea of similarity they encode. For the adherents of grammaticalization theory, the attractiveness of this innovation lies in the reanalysis of the morphosyntactic profile of verbal items. Apparently, new semantic values may be described in terms of the drift of the inflectional forms of *DIRE* from a straightforwardly lexical (or content) to a more discourse-internal one. Indeed, the role of linking a premise and what it might suggest or bring to mind makes conditional forms similar to some adverbs and conjunctions. This is evidenced by the examples below. They have all been drawn from the *TLFi* corpus; the symbol => stands for 'synonymous with'.

(3a) *C'est vitreux, mou, aveugle, bordé de rouge,* **on dirait** *des écailles de poisson* (Sartre, *Nausée*, 1938, p. 33) 'It's glassy, soft, blind, rimmed with red, kind of fish scales' => **comme** *des écailles*.

(3b) **On aurait dit que** *Robert avait entendu le murmure de mes pensées* (Beauvoir, *Mandarins*, 1954, p. 335) 'It was as if Robert had caught the murmur of my train of thought' => *Robert* **paraissait** / **avait l'air de** *avoir entendu*.

(3c) *Non pas une part de la moitié, non ... ce serait trop; ... mais,* **comme qui dirait** *une prime de cinquante pour cent* (France, *Jocaste*, 1879, p. 108) 'Not one slice of a half, no ... it would be too much ...., but, a fifty percent bonus, so to speak' => ... *mais,* **plus ou moins** ... .

That is how form-meaning pairs become parts of grammar. Summarizing, the present study focuses on constructions that, in their historical development, lose their erstwhile substance to become increasingly schematic. The process has a clearly directional character and proceeds via a series of incremental micro-steps.

1.3 Reciprocal constructions – semantic types and structural models

A reciprocal construction is a form-meaning pair serving to encode reciprocal relations. Irrespective of its detailed syntactic characteristics (type of clause, omitted or overtly expressed arguments, etc.), it denotes states of affairs with two or more participants (A, B, …) in which the relation between A and B is the same as the relation between B and A (Lichtenberk, 1985: 23–27). Thus, compared to reflexive constructions which express simple situations, the co-indexation in reciprocal constructions is slightly more complicated: rather than operating between the sets as wholes, reciprocity relates their particular members one by one. Such form-meaning pairs are minimally required to state how participants happen to be put in correspondence. The following Portuguese example illustrates how a bare predicate (with no arguments being present) can succeed in making this minimal variant discursively viable.

(4) **Brigaram**, *mas já se reconciliaram* literally: Quarrelled, but already reconciled 'They have quarrelled but made amends ever since'

Although participants' names can frequently be omitted in null-subject languages (as in example 4), rules of syntactic completeness may require certain slots to be filled with arguments as well. Another circumstance licensing the deletion of at least one argument involves situations in which its referent can either be identified on contextual basis (see 5a) or its mention is simply immaterial. Finally, empty slots abound in underspecified or habitual sentences (see 5b).

(5a) *Casou com ela* literally: got married with her, i.e. 'He got married with her'
(5b) *Paul se marie sur un coup de tête* 'Paul gets married simply if he feels like doing so'

Depending on the type of relation and semantic properties of the predicate, yet another element, the reciprocal marker, may be needed or not. In the first place, instances of its being absent are common in sentences built on inherent reciprocal predicates. Units belonging to this class of signs denote symmetric relations (as *brigar, casar* and *se marier* in the examples above) and are sometimes classified as 'lexical reciprocals'. Indeed, their very meaning already has a reciprocal character, thus warranting no additional grammatical marking. Symmetric predicates consist of a semantically restricted, yet morphologically very heterogeneous, set of expressions whose denotations fall generally into one of the four groups: social relations ('flirt', 'quarrel', 'friend'), spatial relations ('adjoin', 'next to'), verbal contact ('converse', 'negotiate') and relations of identity or non-identity ('same as', 'different from', 'resemble'). In a cross-linguistic perspective, the presence of inherent reciprocal expressions is sometimes held to represent one of the lexical universals. Indeed, hardly can any language be figured out with no lexemes denoting such concepts as otherness, sameness, friendship, company, talk, neighbour, agreement, or contact. All of them are symmetric relations.

Concepts of this kind constitute only a subclass of reciprocal states of affairs. They are different from the remaining reciprocal relations in that the situations they denote can be diagrammatically represented as: $x\ R\ y \to y\ R\ x$. Simplifying somewhat, one token of a given relation suffices to put the two participants in a mutual correspondence (i.e. in both directions). Their ordering is such that x is the starting point (or the domain) of a relation, with y being its endpoint (the range) and, at the same time, y is the starting point, with x being the endpoint. Thus, what is being dealt with here is a purely lexical method of encoding reciprocity. Of course, not all types of reciprocal relations are symmetric. Unlike in the previous case, in *The people on the bus waved at us and we waved back*, there are at least two, perhaps not simultaneous, tokens of waving (one-way waving is possible, one-way marriage is by far more problematic). It must be stressed that symmetry is not always at odds with the presence of specialized reciprocal exponents. Yet, if grammatical marking is found in company of expressions belonging to this class, its contribution is slightly different from what markers habitually perform in ordinary reciprocal constructions (see below).

Second, grammatical marking can also be done away with in some constructions that do not rely on inherent reciprocal predicates. Unlike symmetric relations, they involve at least two relation-tokens of the same nature. Each of them puts the same set of participants in correspondence. Yet, participants are inversely ordered in each of the occurrences of a given relation-token. If speakers opt for encoding the parts of such relations by means of separate clauses, iconic bi-clausal combinations appear and specialized reciprocal marking is no longer needed. Multiclausal sequences are often truncated by omitting the verb in the second clause (this is sometimes called *gapping*). As a consequence, there are not two syntactically autonomous constructions any longer (capable of standing alone in a discourse sequence). Two Old French sentences depict this particular case:

> (6a) *Qant messire Gauvains l'esgarde, D'aler contre li ne se tarde, Si la salue et ele lui*, Cligès, v.3551–3552 (DÉCT) 'Once sire Gauvain sees her, He cannot resist moving towards her; He greets her and so does she'
> (6b) *Vos confondez lui et il vos* RdT, v. 7559 (LFA) 'You are disconcerting him, and vice-versa'

In modern Romance languages, where clitics and clitic clusters are strongly dependent on the presence and the form of the verb, straightforward (i.e. with no gapping), multiclausal combinations are relatively rare. The lack of syntactic, morphological and prosodic autonomy of pronouns minimizes the likelihood of such discourse units (see, for example, Martins, 2014: 49–50). In medieval texts, by contrast, multiple clauses being juxtaposed to convey reciprocity used to be less constrained. Their presence or absence was dictated mainly by practical or discourse-organization factors: sequential alignment of the same lexical material was frequently at variance with the general tendency to avoid repetition. Another compelling reason for the relative rarity of such constructions is that they are well-suited to bring together exactly two relations of the same kind. If more events are to be represented with no prejudice for meaning, the sequence runs the risk of turning into a tedious enumeration. Be that as it may, the fact is that no language relying solely on multiclausal constructions is reported in typological literature. Therefore, other solutions enabling speakers to encode reciprocity with no grammatical means are applied. It is not infrequent that the second clause is substituted with *vice-versa*, or units synonymous with it. All of them are used felicitously only to reciprocalize ordinary (i.e. non-symmetric) relations. Their function is to signal that the same state of affairs as the one that has just been mentioned is introduced anew in the discourse, but participants act on each other in an inverted order, defined in terms of domain and range.

Finally, one more type of reciprocal sequences with no overt marking is marginally attested. Actually, their semantic status is unclear. Like multiclausal constructions, they are built on non-symmetric predicates. As a result, the interpretation according to which participants A and B are only casually involved in the same type of activity, without being reciprocally related, is not unlikely. The point is that the predicate denotes states of affairs that are, more frequently than not, thought of as mutual, thus lending support to the usefulness of the concept of so-called 'naturally reciprocal events' (Kemmer, 1993: 17). Even if devoid of grammatical marking, such sentences tend to be viewed as reciprocal. If their subject cannot be omitted, the predicate usually combines with non-singular antecedents.

(7a) *They were in love*
(7b) *Ils ont dansé toute la soirée* 'They were dancing all night long'[6]

---

6   An interesting case of lexically induced reciprocity, determined by the synergistic semantics of both predicate and its arguments and adjuncts, has been extensively discussed by Dalrymple *et alii* (1998: 194). Sentences with *each other*, coined on the basis of at least two anti-symmetric relations are analyzed (with x R y –> y R x being impossible by virtue of the very lexical meaning of the predicate; e.g. if a war is waged prior to a peace treaty, the same treaty cannot be prior to this war). Thus, *The children follow each other into the church* refers to a situation in which the children are traversing

Symmetric predicates have frequently been left out of consideration in debates over linguistic means of encoding reciprocity. And no wonder: one of the characteristics intrinsic to the members of this class is that no method is known to derive them from non-symmetric predicates. Thus, their status departs radically from, for example, causative verbs which can be derived from non-causative ones provided that appropriate grammatical means are used. In so doing, inherent reciprocal predicates look as if they were of little interest to grammarians. What one can be looking forward to at best is coining an ordinary reciprocal construction out of a non-reciprocal predicate (e.g. *admire* vs. *admire each other*). Obviously, the meaning resulting from such additions cannot be equated with a symmetric relation (numerous relation-tokens in the case of *admire each other* vs. single relation-token in *negotiated*).

Yet, not in all respects do lexical reciprocals eschew a systematic grammatical analysis. At least as far as Romance languages are concerned, they do have a bundle of recurrent syntactic features. Unlike in ordinary reciprocal constructions, their arguments can be inserted into two syntactically unequal slots. In such cases, one of the arguments is usually a subject-NP, whereas the second is part of the VP. It surfaces, then, as an oblique NP hierarchically subordinate to the predicate. Frequently, it is introduced via a preposition corresponding to the English 'with'. Such sentences are going to be referred to as 'discontinuous reciprocal constructions'. By default, they are eligible to host inherent reciprocal predicates only.

By contrast, ordinary predicates have their arguments aligned differently. Instead of being distributed over two syntactically unequal slots, these arguments belong to a single non-singular constituent. They surface, then, either as plural NPs (*The boys waved goodbye to each other*) or, otherwise, as members of a coordinate nominal group (*Robert and Paul waved goodbye to each other*). In each of the cases, special reciprocal marking is mandatory. This model is known as 'simple reciprocal construction'. Apart from accommodating ordinary predicates, simple constructions provide a convenient linear template for inherent reciprocal expressions as well (*Landlords and tenants negotiate rents individually*).

---

an elongated path which begins at some spatial point and ends inside another point. There are children in such event that cannot, at the same time, both follow and be followed. Some child must be the first to go into the church, in which case he or she does not follow any other child. Likewise, the last child cannot be said to be followed. By contrast, the distribution of subparts of *follow each other* in *The children followed each other around the Maypole* is different. The divergence is attributed to the circular shape of the path having been traversed. According to the authors, in the latter case 'it is possible for every child to bear *follow* relation to every other child indirectly'.

In addition, the two classes of expressions differ in their behaviour with respect to multiclausal constructions. Inherent symmetric predicates, but not ordinary ones, are precluded from entering them.

(8a) *La beauté de la vielle ville contraste avec la laideur des grands immeubles* 'The beauty of the old town is in contrast with the ugliness of blocks of flats'

(8b) **La beauté de la vielle ville contraste avec la laideur des grands immeubles et la laideur des grands immeubles contraste avec la beauté de la vielle ville* 'The beauty of the old town is in contrast with the ugliness of blocks of flats and the ugliness of blocks of flats is in contrast with the beauty of the old town'

(9a) *Peter and Jacques nodded to each other in agreement*

(9b) *Peter nodded at Jacques and so did Jacques at Peter*

The reasons for the oddness of bi-clausal constructions containing lexical reciprocal predicates lie in the very nature of symmetric relations. As said above, symmetry involves by definition a single state of affairs distributed at once over a given set of participants, thus licensing a reversal of the hierarchy between them. Therefore, the second clause in 8b conveys a superfluous piece of information, thus contravening the rules that govern the course of conversation.

Another problem that calls for an answer is: under what circumstances are inherent reciprocal predicates allowed to co-occur with grammatical exponents inside a single sentence? The point is that the sentences *John and Dolores quarrelled* (simple construction) and *John quarrelled with Dolores* (discontinuous construction) need not be entirely synonymous. Simple constructions, but not the discontinuous ones, exhibit an ambiguity: they might be taken to assert that the individuals named John and Dolores are collectively involved in a quarrel with someone else, whose identity fails to be overtly expressed. This semantic duplicity is to be blamed on the fact that the oblique argument in discontinuous constructions tends sometimes to be omitted. Therefore, language users might be at a loss finding out whether the sentence is complete or not. In the latter case, the string *John and Dolores quarrelled* is a truncated discontinuous construction, i.e. with a zero oblique argument. To obviate this kind of difficulties, simple constructions, in spite of being built on lexical reciprocals, are occasionally complemented with a grammatical marker, eventually producing *John and Dolores quarrelled with each other.*

Thus, except for multiclausal combinations and sentences denoting 'naturally reciprocal states of affairs', ordinary expressions cannot help but combine with grammatical markers to encode reciprocity. If markers are absent, the semantic value of a given sentence is quite different. For example, bare plural forms in *They were laughing* would simply produce the assertion that a certain number of individuals were engaged, either collectively or each on their own, in a particular kind of activity with no interaction being implied. Such a radical meaning shift is to be traced back to the multiplicity of states of affairs being conjoined. This has been cleverly summarized by Haspelmath (2007: 2110) who states: 'Multiplex mutual events can only be expressed by grammatical reciprocals'. The formula in (10) is thought to depict the semantic structure of ordinary reciprocal constructions. The superscript (') is meant to signal that the second relation-token of the same nature is present.

(10) x R y and y R' x[7]

Finally, it remains to be seen why Romance languages, and human languages in general, avail themselves of grammatical means of expressing reciprocity. As suggested by Waltereit (2012: 13–14) for reflexives, from a design point of view, special marking of this semantic value is superfluous in human languages. Indeed, multiclausal constructions are likely to convey this meaning with equal efficiency by simply juxtaposing numerous non-symmetric predicates alongside their arguments in an appropriate order. As for inherent reciprocal predicates, no grammatical marking whatsoever proves necessary. Moreover, while numerous human languages are frequently deprived of seemingly more purposeful categories (for relevant statistics of plural marking, past tense forms, and the encoding of definiteness; see Waltereit, 2012: 14, based on data retrieved from World Atlas of Language Structures Online), reciprocal marking is cross-linguistically very widespread.

Several concurrent factors seem to be at work here. All of them share a functionalist flavour, inasmuch as special reciprocal marking is seen as serving particular aims in communication. A simple economy appears to be an overriding factor that induces speakers to apply markers rather than to build chains consisting of cumbersome circumlocutions with recurrent elements. Moreover, speakers tend

---

7   Likewise, I. Mel'cuk (2006: 215) emphasizes the incremental character of the non-reciprocal > reciprocal meaning shift: according to him, if the overall semantic architecture of a sentence subject to transformation is 'x stands in relation R to y', a new element is added at the outcome: 'at the same time, y stands in relation R to x'. However, Mel'cuk's notation does not go unchallenged. Unlike inherent reciprocity, ordinary reciprocity is taken here to rely on a free-choice conjunction of at least two non-symmetric relations of the same kind (since *I have great respect for him, but he hasn't any for me* is not in itself contradictory, then *We respect each other* is not necessary), some distinction between relation-tokens is needed. Moreover, the formula *at the same time* is somewhat misleading. In fact, the two relations can be arranged sequentially. The sentence *He showed some respect for me first, then I started respecting him in return* can, in retrospect, be felicitously abbreviated as *We respected each other*. Thus, simultaneity is by no means necessary.

to depict mutual states of affairs from the perspective of the entire set of participants, not just from individual participant's point of view (Haspelmath, 2007: 2091). Finally, as said above, multiclausal combinations are well-suited to communicate a conjunction of exactly two situations of the same kind. Yet, if their cardinality exceeds two, their successive enumeration becomes discursively unviable.

1.4 Empirical data

Unless marked otherwise, translations of Romance examples are mine. The sources, both of the original fragments of Latin texts and their translations are indicated in round brackets. Abbreviations are listed separately in references (e.g. 'TLL – The Latin Library' alongside other details). As for the retrieval of Latin and Old Romance data, the task was carried out by simply launching searches in open-source corpora, repositories, and databases. Each quotation contains the indication of the corpus. Their list is, likewise, available at the end of the monograph (e.g. 'DÉCT – Dictionnaire Électronique de Chrétien de Troyes').

Search methods varied according to whether Latin or medieval examples were looked for. Except for this linguistic criterion, the type of reciprocal structure was taken into consideration as well. As for sentences with *alter, alius* and *uter*, which form a closed set, the query was quite simple. If a search engine happened to be available, a lemma, encompassing all inflectional or spelling variants of one of these lexemes, was defined first. Then, results were manually processed to ascertain which occurrence of *alter, alius* and *uter* was immediately followed by another of its inflectional forms. By default, these elements were required to be placed adjacently or to be separated by an insignificant break to their inflectional mate (e.g. *alius ex alio*). Given the presence in late Latin texts of the *alterutrum* marker, search criteria were refined so as to pick out words having *alter* as one of its parts.

Much in the same vein, occurrences of Romance markers dating back to *unus alterum* were retrieved. Corpora were simply scanned for the presence of *autre* (*aultre, altre*, etc. for French), *otro* (for Spanish), or *outro* (for Portuguese). Then, the results were subject to further manual work to discriminate sequences where these elements happened to be in correlation with the descendants of *unus* (again with a multitude of spelling variants).

Slightly different procedures had to be implemented when looking for reciprocal sequences juxtaposing, either contiguously or not, two inflectional forms of the same noun. Unlike pronouns spawning reciprocal markers, common nouns eligible to appear in two-noun clusters form an open set. The task was less complicated in Old Spanish than in Latin. Spanish binominal clusters used to be built nearly exclusively on human-denoting common nouns, preferably in the singular. Thus, the selection of two dozen or so candidates deemed most probable (e.g. *xpistiano, xristiano, omne, uassallo, uezino, vezino, muger, mugier, fidalgo, fijo dalgo*, and so on, once more with numerous spelling variants; the forms are retrieved from the *Ordenamiento de Alcalá*) was expected to bring satisfactory results. Of course, all of the Old Spanish codices quoted in essay 3 were extensively read to retrieve peripherally attested reiterations as well.

By contrast, Latin reiterated clusters involving two forms of a single common noun proved more difficult to come by. The point is that Latin allowed an unconstrained interplay of elements having both animate and inanimate denotata. Likewise, no preferences in the selection of either singular or plural forms were recorded. Finally, on account of the variation in case, two juxtaposed forms never happened to be alike. Thus, the search relied once more on probabilistic criteria. In case of the original version of the Vulgate, the work by Alexander Cruden (1835) containing manually compiled concordances for each lexical element was of great help.

Essay 1. Fluctuations in the Latin reciprocal system

2.1 Reiterated clusters

The expression of reciprocity in Old Romance languages relies prevailingly on sequences that originate from *unus alterum*. The same structural template, where two elements are juxtaposed, is documented on an even larger scale at various stages in the history of Latin. Still, unlike markers in Romance medieval vernaculars where two different items belonging to one series are aligned (thus producing a contrast; see Introduction, ft. 1), reciprocal sequences in Latin are by default based on reiterations: two inflectional forms of a single noun or pronoun are placed adjacently. One of the two neighbouring forms is coerced into taking a particular case value by another element of the sentence. In the first of the examples below, *legere* 'choose, appoint' must have an accusative form as its complement.

The aim of the present essay is to answer the following two questions: 1) how were reiterations replaced with contrast ? and 2) what prompted the reduction of a series of semantically specialized bipartite markers and the emergence of one universal construction? The hypothesis which is going to be advocated here has mainly a chronological dimension: the reanalysis of the syntactic profile of reciprocal clusters dates back to as early as the Latin period itself. If in classical writings reiterations outnumber by far *unus alterum*, in late Latin texts a serious growth of the latter marker is evidenced, obviously at the expense of polyptotic structures. As a result, in the first documents compiled in Romance vernaculars, the only universally attested reciprocal sequence is the descendant of *unus alterum*. Therefore, the shift is presumed to have been prior to the outset of Romance languages.

Following the principles of the directional change parameter, the reiteration > contrast switch will be demonstrated to have proceeded via a series of small-scale steps. Syntactic contexts enabling speakers to go through with the innovation and to eventually dismantle the classical system are going to be highlighted throughout. Crucial facts revolve around the shifts that affected three segments of the classical Latin grammar: the erosion of some of the morphologically marked number contrasts, speakers' tendency to regularize the expression of NP referential properties, as well as an interchangeable use of various reciprocal clusters. As a consequence, Latin bipartite sequences ended up replaced with constructions relying on non-reiterated exponents. These three general developmental trends are assumed to represent the starting points for the ultimate collapse of the architecture of Latin reciprocity.

At first sight, Latin reciprocal clusters constitute an impeccable series of semantically well-defined and not overlapping form-meaning correspondences. Each of them is different from their counterparts in that it fulfils a separate set of semantic criteria. The selection of the appropriate construction is dependent upon the following binary features: (a) temporarily circumscribed vs. timeless character of the state of affairs denoted; (b) quantifying force of elements denoting reciprocally related participants: nominal items with presupposition of existence are contrasted with non-specifically used nouns; (c) the exact number of participants being involved: two vs. more than two. The first of these criteria is rarely independent from the second (but not the other way round). Indeed, states of affairs represented as taking place at no specific moment or time interval are usually paired with virtual participants (Corbett, 2000: 19). Rather than referring, the nouns that denote them introduce concepts in discourse: they elucidate what features are sufficient to qualify as e.g. *miles* 'soldier' in the second example (to be of age, to be male, to be entitled to receive a salary, to live encamped, and so on). By contrast, the speaker does not commit himself as to the existence of specific soldiers, be they real or imaginary. No individual cases are being dealt with here. The intersection of these criteria is at the basis of at least[8] three types of reiterated reciprocal clusters:

- constructions where two different case forms of a single common noun are juxtaposed to introduce relations with no temporal anchorage and with non-specific participants. Individuals and objects involved in this kind of relations are required to be similar enough to be subsumed under the scope of one lexical element. Importantly, this formal template has enough resiliency to accommodate nouns in both the singular and the plural. Likewise, both human-denoting items and nouns denoting inanimate objects are allowed to appear in such sequences. The pertinence of this peculiar trait of two-noun clusters will be discussed at some length in essay 3.

---

8   In classical Latin, one more reiterated sequence, *uter utrum*, with a reciprocal interpretation is evidenced. Unlike its three counterparts referred to above, it is seemingly limited to embedded clauses (mainly indirect questions). Cf. ... *neque diiudicari posset,* **uter utri** *virtute anteferendus videretur.* Cæs., *BG* 5, 44, 13 (TLL) 'nor could it be determined which of the two appeared worthy of being preferred to the other' (transl. PG); *reliquum est, iudices, ut nihil iam quaerere aliud debeatis, nisi* **uter utri** *insidias fecerit* Cic., *Mil* 23 IX 23 (TLL) 'O judges, that you have now nothing else to inquire into but which plotted against the other' (transl. LC). Its historical significance is that *uter* gave rise in the subsequent stages of Latin to another hybrid bipartite marker *alteruter*.

(1a) *et ad Vadimonis lacum Etrusci lege sacrata coacto exercitu, cum **vir virum** legisset, quantis nunquam alias ante simul copiis simul animis dimicarunt* Livy UC 9, 39, 5 (TLL) 'Besides this the Etrurians, having raised an army under the sanctions of the devoting law, when each man appoints another, came to an engagement at the Cape of Vadimon, with more numerous forces' (PG)

(1b) *Curam acuebat quod adversus Latinos bellandum erat, lingua, moribus, armorum genere, institutis ante omnia militaribus congruentes: **milites militibus, centurionibus centuriones, tribuni tribunis** compares collegaeque iisdem [in] praesidiis, saepe iisdem manipulis permixti fuerant* Livy UC 8, 6, 15 (TLL) 'What excited their attention particularly was, that they had to contend against Latins, who coincided with themselves in language, manners, in the same kind of arms, and more especially in military institutions; soldiers had been mixed with soldiers, centurions with centurions, tribunes with tribunes, as comrades and colleagues, in the same armies, and often in the same companies' (PG)

(1c) ***Vir viro, armis arma*** *conserta sunt* Curtius Rufus, *Hist* 3, 2, 13 (TLL) '(in a phalanx), man stands close to man, weapons are joined to weapons' (HTH)

(1d) ***ferrum ferro*** *acuitur et homo exacuit faciem amici sui*, Vulg. *Num* 27, 17 (BGW - BSV) 'Iron sharpens iron, so a man sharpens the countenance of his friend' (BGW - KJV)

– constructions where two different case forms of *alter* (e.g. *alter*.NOM *alterum*. ACC) are juxtaposed to introduce time-specific relations involving exactly two participants (individual or collective), generally denoted by specifically used nouns appearing in the preceding stretches of the same text

(2a) *Sic fortuna in contentione et certamine utrumque versavit, ut **alter alteri** inimicus auxilio salutique esset.* Cæs. *BG* 5, 44, 13 (TLL) 'Fortune so dealt with both in this rivalry and conflict, that the one competitor was a succour and a safeguard to the other' (PG)

(2b) *Nec ego illi gratiam debeo nec ille mihi poenam: **alter ab altero** absoluitur* Sen., *Benef* 6, 5, 1 (PER) 'I do not owe you gratitude, nor do you owe me compensation - each is cancelled by the other' (PG)

(2c) *non abscisum in duas partes exercitum, cum **altera alteri** auxilium ferre non posset* Cæs. *Civ* 3, 72 (TLL) 'and the separation of the army into two parts, so that the one could not give relief to the other' (PG)

(2d) *deinde aequitate iustitiaque gaudebunt, omniaque **alter pro altero** suscipiet, neque quicquam unquam nisi honestum et rectum **alter ab altero** postulabit* Cic. *Læ* 82 (LC) 'they will delight in what is equitable and accords with law, and will go to all lengths for each other; they will not demand from each other anything unless it is honourable and just' (LC)

(2e) *nec id accusatores magis arguere quam fateri reos, qui noxii ambo **alter in alterum** causam conferant*, Liv. UC 5, 11, 6 (TLL) 'and this their accusers were not more forward to maintain than the defendants to confess, who, equally guilty, threw the blame on one another' (PG)

- constructions where two different case forms of *alius* (e.g. *alius*.NOM *alium*. ACC) are juxtaposed to introduce time-specific relations involving more than two participants

(3a) ***Alius ex alio*** *causam tumltus quaerit* Cæs. *BG* 6, 37, 6 (TLL) 'and one inquires of another the cause of the confusion' (PG)

(3b) ... *atque* ***alios alii*** *deinceps exciperent, integrique et recentes defetigatis succederent* Cæs. *BG* 5, 16, 4 (TLL) 'and then the one relieved the other, and the vigorous and fresh succeeded the wearied' (PG)

(3c) *In primis hoc volunt persuadere, non interire animas, sed ab* ***aliis*** *post mortem transire* ***ad alios****, atque hoc maxime ad virtutem excitari putant metu mortis neglecto* Cæs. *BG* 6, 14, 6 (TLL) 'They wish to inculcate this as one of their leading tenets, that souls do not become extinct, but pass after death from one body to another, and they think that men by this tenet are in a great degree excited to valour, the fear of death being disregarded' (PG)

(3d) *atque in magistratus uersi circumspectant ora principum* ***aliorum alios*** *intuentium fremuntque adeo perditas res desperatumque de re publica esse ut nemo audeat in Hispaniam imperium accipere* Liv. *UC* 26, 18 (TLL) 'turning towards the magistrates, they looked round at the countenances of their most eminent men, who were earnestly gazing at each other, and murmured bitterly, that their affairs were in so ruinous a state, and the condition of the commonwealth so desperate, that no one dared undertake the command in Spain' (PG)

(3e) *tres duces discordantes prope ut* ***defecerint alii ab aliis****, trifariam exercitum in diuersissimas regiones distraxere.* Liv. *UC* 26, 41 (TLL) 'their three generals, having differed so far as almost to have abandoned each other, have divided their army into three parts, which they have drawn off into regions as remote as possible from each other' (transl. PG)

(3f) *Tum* ***alii alios*** *hortari ut repeterent pugnam,* Liv. *UC* 10, 36 (TLL) 'The men then began to encourage each other to return to the battle' (transl. PG)

The efficiency of such a method of expressing reciprocity hinges crucially on variation in case. Not only do inflectional contrasts set apart two adjacent elements formally, but they also show how pronouns found in the *alter alterum* and *alius alium* clusters are anaphorically related to what they happen to co-refer with. Indeed, pronominal forms in Latin reciprocal constructions behave as substitutes of previously mentioned verbal arguments (see 4a–b with antecedents given in bold italics). Besides, it must be stressed that Latin noun inflection is cumulative: aside from lexical content, each inflectional variant carries multiple functional features at the same time. Both are associated with a single morphological segment (e.g. inflectional ending alongside stem alternation). For example, *militibus* in 1a represents simultaneously the dative case and the plural.

(4a) *in quo quid potest esse mali, cum mors nec ad **vivos** pertineat nec ad **mortuos**? **Alteri** nulli sunt, **alteros** non attinget* Cic. Tusc. 1, 38, 91–92 (TLL) And in this state of things where can the evil be, since death has no connection with either the living or the dead? The former have no existence at all, the latter are not yet affected by it (PG; the choice is left only between the living and the dead ones).

(4b) ***Milites** Romani, perclusi tumultu insolito, arma capere **alii, alii** se abdere, pars territos confirmare, trepidare omnibus locis* Sall., Jug. 38, 5 (TLL) The Roman soldiers were alarmed with an unusual disturbance; some of them seized their arms, others hid themselves, others encouraged those that were afraid; but consternation prevailed everywhere (PG; at least three classes of soldiers are singled out according to what their reactions are)

Apart from relying on cumulative inflectional distinctions, Latin reiterated clusters are themselves cumulative. They synthesize reciprocity and two other kinds of information: specificity vs. non-specificity (or, in Haspelmath's terms, the unique identifiability of the referent or its lack; see Haspelmath, 1997: 38) and numeric quantification.

As for the first of these functional features, its lack of morphological marking in Latin is made up for by rigorous constraints affecting the selection of lexical material in reciprocal clusters. The second semantic dimension is tripartite: exactly two *vs.* more than two *vs.* no matter how many (for two-noun sequences). The distinction between binary quantification and generalized plural is morphologically (i.e. word-internally) marked, yet to a limited extent only. In classical Latin, the first of these semantic values is paired with the *-t(e)r* affix. Rather unsurprisingly, *alter* is known to exhibit etymological links with *aut*, an exclusive disjunction ('either … or', 'one of the two, but not both' as distinct from *uel* 'or' in 'one of the two, or both' whose origin is to be traced back to *volo, volui, velle* 'to want'; Traina & Bertotti, 1985: 180–183). Aside from *alter*, this affix is found in some of the comparative forms of adjectives (unlike *dexter* 'right-hand', which implies that exactly two objects are involved, the superlative *dextĭmus* 'the rightmost' is predicated only after more than two items are involved), *neuter* 'none of the two' vs. *nullus* 'nobody, irrespective of how many individuals there can be'.

2.2 First symptoms of the breakdown of the classical system

The three form-meaning pairs described above began receding long before the rise of the Romance languages. After the disappearance of their semantic specialization, the process reaches its peak with the emergence of a series of new reciprocal constructions. Unlike their classical forerunners, the resulting markers do not exhibit cumulative character any longer. Their unique task is to express reciprocity.

The shift comes about after two systemic properties of the classical Latin grammar are modified: binary quantification is done away with and the expression of definite *vs.* indefinite and specific *vs.* non-specific contrasts arises. The first of these changes can be traced back to the influence of language-internal mechanisms. By contrast, the birth of articles is an instance of contact-induced grammatical innovation.

The three-way distinction inside the category of number becomes simplified. In late Latin writings, only the singular and the plural are found. Curiously, the surviving form for the generalized plural (no matter how many objects short of one) is *alter*, the former exponent of the dual. By contrast, *alius* fails to carry over into the emergent Romance languages. According to A. Meillet (1904/1905: 9), this functional impoverishment was triggered by contextual factors: 'ils [certain shifts] proviennent de la structure de certaines phrases, où tel mot paraît jouer un rôle spécial'. The neutralization of the dual *vs.* plural division is very well evidenced particularly under the scope of negation. Meillet cites a sentence by Ovid *neque enim spes altera restat* to corroborate the influential role of the syntactic setting. The sentence can be translated indiscriminately either as 'no second hope is left' or as 'no other hope is left'. The entailment found behind this solution is as follows: since the only available hope is definitely gone, it no longer matters how many other instances, two or more, would have been there. The phenomenon is reported to be neatly attested as early as in Classical Latin (Bertocchi *et alii*, 2010: 156–162).

(5a) ... *neque Capuae neque ullius alterius rei memor* Livy UC 26, 8, 2 (TLL) 'irrespective of whether one might have in mind Capua or whatever other concern' (PG)

(5b) *Cum autem virtutibus inter se sit concordia nec ulla altera melior aut honestior sit, quædam tamen quibusdam personis aptior est* Sen., *Clem* 1, 5, 3 (LC) 'Though, moreover, the virtues are at harmony with each other, and no one of them is better or more noble than another, yet to certain people a certain virtue will be more suited' (LC)

It remains to elucidate how this shift subsequently spread to other contexts. Meillet cleverly eschews the question, by simply stating that 'cette valeur a été transportée dans des phrases quelconques, et les langues romanes, laissant tomber *alius*, n'ont conservé que *alter*, pour exprimer le sens de autre' (1904/1905: 10; 'this value spilled over to any type of sentences and Romance languages, after *alius* had been eliminated, kept *alter* as the unique form to convey the idea of otherness'). According to P. Tekavčić (1980: 159), language users perceive contrasts between two objects as more salient than contrasts where one out of many (more than two) comparable objects – colours, shapes, figures, words – is to be singled out. Indeed, binary divisions have been demonstrated to be processed at a higher speed (Humphreys & Quinlan, 1987: 48–64; Kveraga *et alii*, 2007: 13232–13233). Proof of this is the average response time in elicited tasks aimed at recognizing the appropriate candidate. Speakers' reactions are quicker for binary contrasts, as they call for a lesser perceptual and/or cognitive effort. The same line of reasoning applies in the domain of reciprocity. It is pairs rather than *n*-tuples (*n*>2) that represent the default option. Instead of being classified according to the accurate number of their parts, reciprocal relations are essentially viewed as consisting of two events of the same kind. No wonder that clusters with *alius* are gradually superseded by variants containing *alter*.

The loss of the classical 'exactly two' vs. 'more than two' distinction under the scope of negation must not be equated with the idea that *alius* is immediately doomed to vanish. In point of fact, the division of labour between the two expressions withstood the ongoing semantic erosion for long. A thorough examination of Latin texts shows that before the eventual decline of *alius* and the advent of *alter* as an all-encompassing expression for the concept of otherness, the two signs went through a stage of interchangeable use. Their competition is confirmed by the recurrent use of *alius* as late as in the Vulgate in contexts unmistakably referring to exactly two participants. Inconsistent uses of this kind can be found sporadically in earlier texts, as well (see the quotation from Livy in 6c below). Interestingly, the opposite situation, i.e. attestations of *alter* when undisputedly more than two objects are involved, is reported outside the functional domain of reciprocity, as well (Bertocchi *et alii*, 2010: 160–162; see 6d).

(6a) *currebant autem **duo** simul et **ille alius discipulus** praecucurrit citius Petro et venit primus ad monumentum* Vulg. *John*, 20, 4 (BGW - BSV) 'And they both ran together: and that other disciple did outrun Peter and came first to the sepulchre' (BGW - KJV)

(6b) *et ego rogabo Patrem et **alium paracletum** dabit vobis ut maneat vobiscum in aeternum* Vulg. *John*, 14, 16 (BGW - BSV) 'And I will ask the Father: and he shall give you another Paraclete, that he may abide with you for ever' (BGW - KJV)

(6c) *Nam **alia parte** ipse adortus est, **alia** Campani omnes, equites peditesque, et cum iis Punicum praesidium cui Bostar et Hanno praeerant erupit* Livy UC 26, 5 (TLL) 'for on one side he himself attacked them suddenly, and on the other side all the Campanians sallied forth, both foot and horse, joined by the Carthaginian garrison under the command of Bostar and Hanno' (PG)

(6d) *snper* [sic!] *arti culum cutem aperiebis et de **tribus nervis** super **alterum** intro haerentibus unum medianum ferramento praecidis, sic ne **alteros nervos** laedas* Mulomedicina Chironis 623, XXXIV (FGB) 'over the finger, you will make a small incision and, out of three nerves adjacent one to the other inside, you will cut the central one so that the remaining nerves are not injured' (translation mine)

It might be concluded, then, that the distinction between *alter alterum* and *alius alium*, although still present in late Latin, was in the process of ceasing to be felt as relevant. Indeed, instances of confusion between reciprocal clusters are easily detectable. Not only did such 'misuses' contribute to weakening formal divisions between bipartite sequences, but, more importantly, they illustrate how semantic boundaries between these sequences were becoming blurred. The stage was thus set for a radical reanalysis of the system. Various cases can be adduced to show how the collapse proceeded. For the aims pursued here, one kind of inconsistencies is of special interest: generic (or habitual, or potential) states of affairs paired with series of pronouns (7a–b)[9].

(7a) *Miluo est quoddam bellum quasi naturale cum corvo ; ergo* **alter alterius** *ubicumque nanctus est ova frangit* Cic. *Nat* 2, 125, 4–6 'The kite and the crow live in a state of natural war as it were with one another, and therefore each destroys the other's eggs wherever it finds them' (PG)

(7b) *Fallacia* **alia aliam** *trudit: iam susurrari audio civem Atticam esse hanc.* Ter. *Andria* 4, 5 v.778–780 (LC) 'One scheme brings on another. I now hear it whispered about that she is a citizen of Attica' (LC)

(7c) *Inde ista tanta coacervatio* **aliorum super alios** *ruentium. Quod in strage hominum magna evenit,* Sen. *De vita beata* VII, 4 (LC) 'The result of this is that people are piled high, one above another, as they rush to destruction. And just as it happens that in a great crush of humanity'(LC)

2.3 Concurrent reciprocal markers

Moreover, bipartite sequences are not the only method of expressing reciprocity. Latin grammar takes advantage of as many as three other signs to achieve the same semantic effect. As said above, the effectiveness of reiterated clusters hinges on inflectionally marked case distinctions. Yet, the Latin case marking is known

---

9 The opposite situation, i.e. instances of specific constructions relying on two-noun clusters, is not convincingly documented in the corpus compiled for the present study. Yet, in some time-honoured Latin textbooks (Menge, 1900: 163–164), reciprocal constructions built with e.g. *alius alium* or *inter se* (see below) are given a parallel, putatively equivalent, version with two inflectional forms of the same noun being juxtaposed. Cf. *Homines inter se* (or *alius alium* or *alii alios*) *amare debent* (or *homo hominem amare debet*); *Milites ad virtutem inter se* (*alius alium*) *cohortati sunt* (or *Miles militem ad virtutem cohortatus est*). Such substitutions, if they were indeed practised, are indicative of a less rigorous partition between Latin reciprocal sequences than it might seem at first sight. Formal likeness of reiterated constructions might have induced speakers to disregard semantic constraints associated with them. Reciprocity, i.e. the most general meaning shared by all polyptotic sequences, was the only criterion.

to have been less rigorously applied in everyday speech than in literary texts, which eventually resulted in the collapse of declensions (see Cravens, 2002: 51–56 for an exhaustive presentation of the phenomenon). Thus, the situation found in the *sermo vulgaris* is sometimes at odds with the need to align two different forms of the same element (Lloyd 1987/1993: 248–254) to produce a reciprocal sequence. By contrast, the remaining methods of encoding this semantic value rely to a lesser extent on inflectional variation than bipartite sequences do. For example, no morphological case marking is needed in the adverb *invicem* 'mutually, reciprocally'. Likewise, the prepositional phrase *inter se* varies only with respect to what grammatical person is dealt with (*inter nos, inter vos* being appropriate for 1.PL and 2.PL respectively). In the adjective *mutuus*, case distinctions do play a role. Yet, in reciprocal constructions this item inflects prevalently as a target of agreement triggered by a nominal head (Kibort, 2010: 78). Thus, the burden of being morphologically marked falls mainly on the noun that *mutuus* happens to determine. All in all, it comes as no surprise that these linguistic signs are used interchangeably with reiterated sequences to convey the same meaning.

The theoretical significance of multiple-choice expression of a single semantic value lies in that it is likely to undermine grammar's stability. This assumption is in line with the functionalist and typological perspectives on why human grammars happen to be reorganized at all (Croft, 2003: 102–107). The interplay of economy and iconicity is viewed as the major driving force responsible for grammatical shifts. A number of semantic relations between linguistic signs - polysemy, homonymy, monosemy, and synonymy – are characterized in terms of being to varying degrees iconic and / or economic. From this point of view, the existence of synonymous lexical units and form-meaning pairs is in keeping with neither of the two tendencies. Iconicity is violated, for there is no one-to-one correspondence between the repertoire of constructions and the inventory of meanings (or functional features) to be transmitted. The disrespect of economy is due to the fact that one of the members of a synonymous pair of linguistic signs is actually superfluous, or communicatively redundant. It does not contribute to satisfying communicative needs of language speakers in a more efficient way. In point of fact, genuine synonyms are hard to come by. Admittedly, in nearly each of the purported pairs, some specialization is found, be it stylistic, regional or in terms of connotations.

In what follows, an attempt is going to be made to show in what respects the three other expressions are functionally similar to bipartite clusters. The adjective *mutuus*, which in nearly all of the retrieved examples is syntactically subordinate to a noun denoting a pragmatically controlled object, is documented mainly in possessive reciprocal constructions. Its role is to emphasize that this 'controlled object' is subject to an exchange. Thus, at least two individuals are represented as reciprocally related. No semantic difference whatsoever is recorded between sentences with *mutuus* and the *alter alterius* – noun sequence (see 8a–b). Of course, unlike bipartite clusters, *mutuus* remains neutral with respect to the type of predication; it is used for both specific and non-specific states of affairs. For example, 9a depicts the fate that is to befall human beings by the will of the ruthless god Mars. If contextual support is sufficient, in sentences with reflexive pronouns accompanying verbs that denote actions involving exchange (hence, carried out by more people), *mutuus* is likely to enhance a reciprocal rather than reflexive value of the pronoun (see 9c).

(8a) *Atque etiam ipsi inter se censores sua iudicia tanti esse arbitrantur ut alter **alterius iudicium** non modo reprehendat, sed etiam rescindat* Cic. *Pro Aulo Cluentio* 122 (LC) 'And lastly, the censors themselves have time after time thrown over the verdicts - if you wish to call them such - of their predecessors' (LC)

(8b) *si ergo ego lavi vestros pedes Dominus et magister et vos debetis alter **alterius** lavare **pedes*** Vulg. *John*, 13, 14 (BGW - BSV) 'If then I being your Lord and Master, have washed your feet; you also ought to wash one another's feet'(BGW - KJV)

(9a) *Iam gravis aequabat luctus et **mutua** Mavors **funera**; caedebant pariter pariterque ruebant victores victique, neque his fuga nota neque illis* Verg., *Aen* 10, 755–757 (TLL) 'Thus Mars relentless holds in equal scale slaughters reciprocal and mutual woe; the victors and the vanquished kill or fall in equal measure; neither knows the way to yield or fly' (PG)

(9b) *Pro eo supplementum ipse ex Africa maxime iaculatorum levium armis petiit, ut Afri in Hispania, in Africa Hispani, melior procul ab domo futurus uterque miles, velut **mutuis pigneribus** obligati stipendia facerent* Livy, *UC* 21, 21, 11 'For this purpose he requested a reinforcement from Africa, chiefly of light-armed spearmen, in order that the Africans might serve in Spain, and the Spaniards in Africa, each likely to be a better soldier at a distance from home, as if bound by **mutual pledges**' (PG)

(9c) *Iam **mutuis** amplexibus et festinantibus saviis **sese** perfruuntur et illae sedatae lacrimae postliminio redeunt prolectante gaudio* Apul., *Met* 5, 7, 5 (TLL) 'There the sisters embraced with eager kisses and took delight of one another, till the tears they had dried welled forth again' (FGB)

Likewise, no clearly defined semantic criteria help circumscribe the exact contribution of *inter se*. Reciprocity appears to be its only semantic characteristic. No additional meaning, be it formulated in terms of referential properties of the elements of a given construction or in terms of the number of participants, is found[10]. The pronoun in this prepositional phrase is required to co-index other

---

10 In Binding Theory, reciprocals alongside reflexives are claimed to be subject to so-called Principle A dealing with local binding, i.e. items whose antecedents are located in a

elements in the same text. As *inter se*, unlike *inter nos* (see 10a), appears both in specific and non-specific reciprocal constructions, anaphoric relations involving *se* are twofold: binding and co-reference (Haegeman, 1994: 205–206). Apart from being the only reciprocal marker in a sentence, *inter se* frequently looks as if it were superimposed onto an already reciprocal form-meaning pair. It is found alongside bipartite clusters (see 10b–c) or *invicem* (10d).

(10a) *Hoc enim uno praestamus vel maxime feris, quod conloquimur **inter nos** et quod exprimere dicendo sensa possumus* Cic. *Ora* I, 32 (TLL) 'For the one point in which we have our greatest advantage over the brute creation is that we hold converse one with another, and can reproduce our thought in word' (PG)

(10b) *... placet Stoicis, quae in terris gignantur, ad usum hominum omnia creari, **homines** autem **hominum** causa esse generatos, ut ipsi **inter se aliis alii** prodesse possent* Cic. *Off* 1, 7, 22 (PG) 'As the Stoics hold, everything that the earth produces is created for man's use; and as men, too, are born for the sake of men, that they may be able mutually to help one another' (PG)

(10c) *... omniaque **alter pro altero** suscipiet, neque quicquam umquam nisi honestum et rectum **alter ab altero** postulabit, neque solum colent **inter se** ac diligent sed etiam verebuntur.* Cic. *Læl* 82 '(LC) ... and, next, they will delight in what is equitable and accords with law, and will go to all lengths for each other; they will not demand from each other anything unless it is honourable and just, and they will not only cherish and love, but they will also revere, each other' (LC)

(10d) *... cum **inter se** innexi rami uinculum **in uicem** praebeant ...* Livy *UC* 33, 5, 12 (TLL) 'the branches thus intertwined, and which mutually bind each other' (PG)

Little space is going to be devoted to the adverb *invicem* 'in turn', 'on alternate occasions' and, from Livy onwards (Pinkster, 2015: 276), 'mutually', 'reciprocally'. For it has a non-nominal character, it is not eligible at all for an analysis conducted within the Government and Binding framework. If inserted in sentences containing the reflexive *se, sui* or *sibi* and referring to an action that implies the

---

nearby context (usually inside the same sentence or clause) and surface e.g. as overtly expressed subjects. This decision seems to be biased in two ways. First, constraints picked out in configurational languages (frequently exemplified with how English reflexives co-index fully-fledged NPs) are given preference in this framework. Second, the relevance of Principle A to the analysis of reciprocal markers can be traced back to the fact that reciprocal relations are strictly predicate-bound. Yet, Latin data appear to be more variegated. For example, bipartite pronominal sequences seem unconstrained in choosing their governing category. By contrast, two-noun sequences can easily be construed as two R-expressions producing a single marker, which means that they are suitably accommodated by Principle C. The prepositional phrase *inter se* seems to be the only marker to be really under the requirement of obeying locality constraints (Haegeman, 1994: 273, 341–343).

co-involvement of many participants, the function of *invicem* is to enhance the reciprocal value of the pronoun. As was the case with *mutuus*, it frequently appears in the company of other markers (see 11a). Regardless of the fact that it does away with the need of being inflected, it is not directly continued in Romance languages.

(11a) *Vixeruntque mira concordia, per* **mutuam** *caritatem, et* **invicem se** *anteponendo* Tac. *Vit. Agr.* VI (ST) 'They lived in singular harmony, through their mutual affection and preference of each other to self' (ST)

(11b) *Ad quas visendas hortandasque cum Alexander veniret, conspectis armatis* **invicem** **se** *amplexae, velut statim moriturae, conplorationem ediderunt* Justin Marcus Iunianius (3rd century A.D.) *Historiarum* 11, IX, 13 (Scuola) 'When Alexander came to see and console them, they threw themselves, at the sight of his armed attendants, into one another's arms, and uttered mournful cries, as if expecting to die immediately' (Tertullian)

2.4 The encoding of NP quantifying force

Another phenomenon which appears to have produced a detrimental effect on the viability of specialized reciprocal form-meaning pairs might be inferred in some of the Roman comedies dating back to as early as the Republican period. First, as their main characters are drawn from common people, their authors tend to imitate the speech of lower social classes. Compared to writings belonging to an elevated style, sentences are relatively simple and short, turn-taking formulae abound (Berger, 2015: 4–5), and the lexicon is by far less sophisticated. Second, the then frequent Greek-Latin bilingualism induces writers and literate readers to appropriate some of the Greek practices found in analogous communicative settings. The innovation is, thus, licensed at first only in very specialized contexts so as to meet expectations of a restricted number of addressees (Matras, 2011: 283). One of the recurrent practices in Hellenic dramas, prolifically imitated in Roman plays, is the tendency to mark NPs' referential status overtly (Penny, 2002: 145). In classical Latin, this feature is known to have no morphological realization. Thus, the case dealt with here may be seen as a contact-induced innovation in grammar. One of the most spectacular examples of this kind of borrowings is evidenced in the *Miles Gloriosus* by Plautus (2nd c. B.C.). The author's idea was to reinstate a Greek humorous play, now lost. Rather than being called with their nicknames, the characters address each other using their functions' names (e.g. 'the-soldier' instead of *Pyrgopolynices*), or nouns simply evoking their physical traits. By these means, numerous occurrences of common nouns are preceded by demonstrative pronouns that are required to agree in number, case and gender with their heads (Bakker, 2009: 9–10). A comparison between

Greek templates and the possibilities offered by Latin grammar appears to have been a necessary step. An attempt was, thus, undertaken to find Latin structures flexible enough to carry the same meaning as in the model language. Indeed, Plautus makes an extensive use of the Hellenic practice of adding demonstratives to common nouns (e.g. v.88 *illest miles*; v.105 *illam amicam*; v.109 *militi huic*; v.110 *illi lenae*; v.111–12 *is ... miles*; v.120 *huic ... militia*; v.127 *illum ... meum rerum*; v.128 *istum militem* ; v.136 *illi amanti suo hospiti*). As a consequence, a real upsurge in demonstratives is recorded in his text. Their frequency seriously exceeds what might be reasonably expected in normal circumstances in Latin. Admittedly, they do not serve the contrastive function any longer; the nouns would suffice to express who is who (see Adams, 2003: 518–519).

As for the mechanism enabling Roman playwrights to replicate the Greek model, various scholars (Diessel, 1999: 115; Diessel, 2006: 469, 472–475; Jungbluth, 2004/2005: 84–85) point to some of the properties of Latin demonstrative pronouns, both singular and plural. If used as heads, they are intrinsically definite and anaphorically point to their left towards an antecedent (as Latin has no special third person personal pronouns, demonstratives can systematically appear in their stead). If used as determiners, they elucidate the status of the NP referent in terms of how it is located with respect to some deictic central point. In doing so, they indicate how the speaker and / or the addressee focus their attention. The spatial value attributed to late Latin demonstrative pronouns, defining the NP referents either as proximal or distal (Marchello-Nizia characterizes this tardy effect in terms of the 'sphère du locuteur', 2006: 116), is still not vivid in Plautus' play. Yet, in the course of time, this function tends to be foregrounded, which eventually results in further refinements of the status of Romance definite articles (Stavinschi, 2012: 75–77). The tendency to achieve this form-function mapping happens to be strengthened by the advent of Christianity, whose sacred books used to be written in Greek (Harrington, 1997: 35).

Aside from setting apart definite and indefinite NPs, emerging articles gradually attain the ability to express another contrast: specific vs. non-specific. The latter functional value takes on the form of bare nouns (Ledgeway, 2011: 412) in Old Romance. As a result, no multiple semantic features, reciprocity alongside (non-)specificity, need be cumulated in a single construction. Instead, their expression becomes split. Encoding reciprocity can be taken care of by any marker ever since, whereas referential contrasts are conveniently associated with articles (on the emergence of the Romance indefinite out of *unus*, see Carlier, 2013: 46–49; Herslund, 2012: 342–343). Once grammar gets rid of cumulative bipartite clusters, the question arises to ascertain how information on the exact cardinality of individuals is conveyed. As said above, *alter* advanced toward the status of generalized plural: irrespective of how many other participants there are, it no longer contrasts with *alius*. The answer is quite simple: numeral expressions are sufficient, as witnessed by 15th century Portuguese examples quoted below.

(12a) *E elles diseram que nã podia ser doutra guissa, por bem e comcordia* **damballas** **partes**, *por verem mais certo que taees eram; deshy espediramse hũs dos outros e foramse* (Fernão Lopes, *CDJI2*, c. CLXXXVIII, 15th century) 'And they said things were unlikely to be different on account of bounty and concord of both parts so that they see it was indeed so; afterwards they left each other and went away'

(12b) *Levavaõ nas cabecas coroas douro ricamemte obradas de pedras dalljofare de grãde preço, naõ imdo arredados huũ do outro, mas* **ambos** *a iguoall* (Fernão Lopes, *CDJI2*, c. XCV) 'They were wearing priceless golden crowns richly wrought with seed pearls, without walking under each other's escort, but on equal terms'

2.5 The career of *unus alterum*

Rather than explaining why it is *unus alterum* and not another expression that ultimately attains the status of an all-encompassing source for Romance markers, the present section traces how it came to reach the dominant position amid a variety of reciprocal markers documented in Latin texts. In classical writings, the attestations of the *unus alterum* sequence are in poor supply. The analysis of the texts compiled before the beginning of the Christian era is suggestive of its pertaining to the spoken register and a less elevated style: it is found either in dialogues imitating everyday speech or in technical treaties. In the scarcely available examples dating back to that period, both parts of *unus alterum* point unambiguously to their left to an antecedent (or a pair of antecedents). In addition, more frequently than not, the sequence under discussion seems to be synonymous with another bipartite reciprocal marker – *alter alterum*. Both of them share the property of having been earmarked for conveying that exactly two entities stand in a reciprocal relation. That is how they were distinct from *alius alium*. Yet, unlike *alter alterum*, which, besides being by far more common, is generally co-indexed with specific antecedents, *unus alterum* is less selective in this respect (see intrinsically specific *nos* in 13a and non-specifically used *iumenta* in 13b). Be that as it may, the fact remains that elements forming both clusters behave as substitutes of verbal arguments. In classical Latin, their interpretation obviously depends upon another element.

(13a) *Verum tempestas memini quom quondam fuit, quom inter* **nos** *sorderemus* **unus** **alteri** Plautus, *Truculentus*, 2, 4, 30 (INTR) 'Indeed, I remember that there was once a time when between ourselves we were loathsome, the one to the other' (archive.org).

Note, in addition, the co-reference between *-emus* of *sorderemus*.1.PL.IMPERF.SUBJ ('to be dirty, be mean, appear worthless') and *unus alteri*

(13b) *eadem ratione **iumenta**, cum iuga eorum subiugiis loris per medum temperantur, aequaliter trahunt onera. cum autem inpares sunt eorum virtutes et **unum** plus valendo premit **alterum** …* Marcus Vitruvius, *De architectura* 10, 8 (1st BC) (penelope) 'Thus also oxen have an equal draft when the piece which suspends the pole hangs exactly from the middle of the yoke. But when oxen are not equally strong …'. (LEX)

In subsequent stages, this fundamental property does not change. For example, the interpretation of the instances of *unus alterum* found in the Vulgate remains strongly dependent on what is dealt with in remaining stretches of the text (see 14a-d; bold elements represent antecedents / postcedents). Still, some innovations do appear. As said above, the collapse of the dual vs. plural distinction results in a gradual decline of *alius alium*. Irrespective of the number of participants, clusters relying on *alter – unus alterum, alterutrum* (see footnote 1 above) and *alter alterum* – gain in frequency at the expense of the erstwhile 'more than two' marker to encode reciprocity. In addition, all of them tend to be used interchangeably. As for *unus alterum*, its former stylistic constraints are removed, which entails a significant increase in the number of its occurrences. This state of affairs marks the dawn of the Romance era.

(14a) *Ioseph lignum Ephraim et **cunctae Israhel sociorumque eius** et adiunge illa **unum ad alterum** tibi in lignum unum et erunt in unionem in manu tua* Vulg. *Ezek.* 37, 16–17 (BGW - BSV) 'For Joseph the stick of Ephraim, and for all the house of Israel, and of his associates. And join them one to the other into one stick, and they shall become one in thy hand' (BGW - KJV)

(14b) *… dicunt **unus ad alterum**, vir ad **proximum suum**, loquentes …* Vulg. *Ezek.* 33, 30 (BGW - BSV) '… and speak one to another each man to his neighbour, saying' (BGW - KJV)

(14c) *Similiter et **summi sacerdotes** ludentes **ad alterutrum** cum scribis dicebant alios salvos fecit se ipsum non potest salvum facere* Vulg. *Mark* 15, 31 (BGW - BSV) 'In like manner also the chief priests, mocking, said with the scribes one to another: He saved others; himself he cannot save' (BGW - KJV)

(14d) *et murmurati sunt contra Mosen et Aaron **cuncti filii Israhel** […] Dixeruntque **alter ad alterum** constituamus nobis ducem et revertamur in Ægyptum* Vulg. *Numbers* 14, 2 & 4 (BGW - BSV) 'All the Israelites grumbled against Moses and Aaron […] And they said one to another: Let us appoint a captain, and let us return into Egypt' (BGW - KJV)

Essay 2. Old French *li uns l'autre*, a multi-faceted reciprocal marker

3.1 One general construction – many detailed problems

In the present essay two evolutionary aspects of Old French (OF) reciprocal sequences are going to be analysed. The central problem in each of them is tied to the presence of the marker originating from the Latin *unus alterum*. The first study attempts to reconstruct the mechanisms responsible for the emergence of cumulative reciprocal sequences. They are peculiar in that the *l'un l'autre* cluster appears alongside the erstwhile reflexive pronoun. The point is that the present day French pattern *Elles s'embrassèrent l'une l'autre sur la joue* 'They kissed each other on the cheeks' paved its way only gradually. In medieval texts, this propositional content used to be expressed either as *Elles s'embrassèrent sur la joue* or *L'une a embrassé l'autre sur la joue*. The French material is thought to lead to a better understanding of the origin of such form-meaning linkages. Compared to reciprocal constructions evidenced in the remaining Romance languages of that period (see Old Spanish examples in 1a-c retrieved from the corpusdelespnol. org, abbrev. CE), the attestations of two etymologically and functionally different items brought together in a unique sentence are relatively tardy in French.

> (1a) *... el lobo & la oueja comerian & beuerian de so vno & non* **se** *farian mal* **el vno al otro** (*Castigos e documentos de Sancho IV*, 13th century; CE) 'The wolf and the sheep will eat and drink from one piece of ware and will avoid causing harm to each other'
>
> (1b) *... que el rrey uenja en tal manera que las gentes* **se** *veyan* **los vnos alos otros** (Anonymous, *Cuento de Tristán de Leonís*, 14th century; CE) '... when the King came so that people could see one another'
>
> (1c) *Quando esto entendieron los Romanos cataron* **se vnos a otros** *entre tanto se juntaron las açes que non ouo y otra falla & metieron las lanças so los braços & fueronse ferir* (*El emperador Otas de Roma*, 14th century; CE) 'Once they understood it, the Romans looked at each other while rallying troops so as not to make another mistake, and they took their lances under their arms and started to wound each other'

The ulterior mind behind this first study is to put to the test the empirical viability of the notions of bridging contexts and subjectification presumed to account for how some constructions come into existence and become grammaticalized over time. Incidentally, issues related to the degree of grammaticalization of reciprocal sequences in various Romance languages are going to be discussed, too.

The second moot point is related to how Latin reiterated two-noun clusters were processed after spoken Latin had become extinct. Seemingly, expressions derived from *unus alterum*, *inter se* and from the syncretic ACC./ABL. forms of the Latin reflexive pronoun cover all the field of formal means of encoding reciprocity in OF. The thing is that, unlike Latin constructions juxtaposing two inflectional forms of the same noun, none of the above-mentioned linguistic signs is earmarked for expressing timeless reciprocal states of affairs with non-specific NPs. Everything looks as if this particular subclass of reciprocal constructions had been done away with altogether, leaving a gap with no special form having been devised in their stead. Nonetheless, in language evolution, shifts generally come about in a more gradual manner (yet, see the discussion in 5.3), which is not in keeping with an abrupt advent of gaps ('New distributions, contexts, and meanings are added to the old ones, which may persist over centuries along with the innovative construction', see Company Company, 2012: 679; Bybee, 2009: 113–114). Therefore, some clues pointing to the survival of the pattern enabling speakers to deal with non-specific, potential reciprocal states of affairs are available. The semantic function under discussion appears to have been carried over to the cluster descending from Latin *unus alterum* as well. The details of how this drift actually took place are going to be unveiled in the second part of the chapter. The fundamental co-reference vs. binding dichotomy (see Büring, 2005: 81–83) will be discussed first, and the whole discussion will, then, move on to the type of anaphoric links exhibited by certain configurations of Old French *l'un l'autre*.

3.2 Semantic variation in the *l'un l'autre* constructions

The changes that *l'un l'autre* underwent (the discussion of its countless spelling variants found in medieval and Renaissance texts has been omitted here) are concomitant to the rise and the subsequent growth in the frequency of the reciprocal *se*. The latter is documented right from the start in OF as a fully-fledged exponent (i.e. one not requiring any other grammatical means) of this semantic value. If *se* enters the prepositional phrase descending from *inter se*, it fails to become definitely fixed in medieval texts, exhibiting variation between a personal pronoun and *sei* (see 2a–b). Moreover, unlike in present-day French, clitic climbing phenomena are triggered in medieval texts in sentences with serial verb constructions (*pouvoir* 'can' and *devoir* 'must' followed by an infinitive or combinations expressing tense and aspect details) containing this pronoun (see 3).

> (2a) … *li prince de la terre ki **entre sei** se cumbatéient* (Anonymous, *Quatre Livres des Rois*, p.6; ARTFL-TFA) '… the dukes of the land who were fighting against each other'
> (2b) *Cil dui plaidierent **entr'els** mout longement* (Anonymous, *Couronnement de Louis* C, v. 2444, 12th century; LFA) 'Those two have been arguing with each other for a very long time'

(3) *Au departir **se corurent besier*** (*Couronnement* ... A1, v. 241; LFA; clitic climbing)
'On the point of leaving, they exchanged kisses with each other'

The interplay of *l'un l'autre* and *se* reshapes their distributional properties, eventually assigning each of them specific discourse values. First of all, these two linguistic signs are mutually exclusive, at least as far as the OF period is concerned. Hardly ever do they appear together to reciprocalize the same predicate. If numerous verbs subject to the non-reciprocal > reciprocal transformation are used in a series, by coordination or in enumerations, it is frequently the case that *l'un l'autre* accompanies one of them, whereas *se* attaches to the next (see 4a-b). The competition goes as far as to extend over the then very widespread class of *entre-* verbs. Disregarding the already reciprocal value of their prefix, they are known to require one more marker. Unlike in contemporary French, there are attestations in medieval texts of both *s'entre-V* or *entre-V l'un l'autre*. Yet, the two grammatical markers fail to appear jointly even with this class of expressions (see 4c-e). Needless to say, various linear configurations of *l'un l'autre* can also convey the meaning under discussion (4f–g). For they are involved in intricate anaphoric relations to their nominal antecedents introduced in preceding (or, sometimes, in the ensuing) parts of the same text, the elements of this bipartite marker behave as if they were substitutes of verbal arguments (Nkollo, 2013b: 17–20). All these cases are represented in the examples below:

- many predicates reciprocalized with different markers each:

  (4a) *Li.j. **va ferir** l'autre; ne se **vont espargnant**: par dessus les hïammes se **vont** maint **cop donnant*** (Anonymous; *Beaudouin de Sebourc*; p. 256; 14th century; ARTFL) 'Without taking care of sparing each other, they are smashing their helmets with rude blows'
  (4b) *Andui joingnent li arrabi, li uns l'autre **pas ne failli**. La ou il primes se troverent, es escuz granz **cox** se **donerent**, la ou li barons s'**entrencontrent**, escuz et hauberz s'**entresfondrent**; de vertu li barons se **fierent**, mes en char pas ne se **toucherent*** (Anonymous; *Roman de Thèbes*; p. 178; 12th century; ARTFL) 'Both of them tighten their spurs, rushing the enemy ardently; as soon as they ran at each other, they stroke terrible blows on each other's shield; once the encounter is under way, knights' helmets and shields are quickly twisted; the lords strike vehemently among themselves, without injuring each other's flesh'

- the *entre-* verb with *se* (without *l'un l'autre*)

  (4c) *Les fers des glaves ont basciés, si s'**entredonent** es escus* (Anonymous, *Vengeance Raguidel*; p. 33; 13th century; ARTFL) 'They lowered the steel of their swords and hit on each other's shields ...'
  (4d) *Bien fierent cist, bien fierent cil, Tost an veïssiez morir mil. Fieremant s'**antreconbatoient*** (Wace, *Partie arthurienne du Roman de Brut*; p. 148; 12th century; ARTFL) 'The ones and

the others gave fierce strikes. You would see them dying by thousands, so bravely did they struggle against one another'

- the *entre-* verb with *l'un l'autre* (without *se*)

(4e) ... *si s'an issent joie feisant et li uns l'autre antrebeisant* (*Érec*, v. 6309–6310; DÉCT) '... they are going out cheerfully, exchanging kisses'

- *l'un l'autre* is the only marker

(4f) ... *ne ne pooit mes gueres nuire li uns a l'autre* (*Érec*, v. 5938–5939; DÉCT) '... nor were they able to cause harm to each other anymore'

(4g) *Ansanble jurent an.i. lit, et li uns l'autre acole et beise: riens nule n'est qui tant lor pleise* (*Érec*, v. 5200–5202; DÉCT) 'They are lying in one bed exchanging hugs and kisses; nothing delights them more than that'

Now, the question to be answered is: how did *l'un l'autre* and *se* become parts of a single highly schematic form-meaning pair, i.e. how did they come to reciprocalize the same predicate? In compliance with a gradualist view of language evolution, the co-occurrence of these two linguistic signs will be demonstrated to have come about via a series of overlapping micro-steps recorded at various levels of linguistic analysis. At the beginning, the only exception comprises a dozen or so verbs of movement (*se partir, se departir, se dessevrer*; see 5a–d).

(5a) *Et il dient qu'il aille en la garde Nostre Seignor, car il dui se partiront le matin li uns de l'autre* (Anonymous, *Queste del Saint Graal*; p. 244; 13th century; ARTFL) 'And they say he should go to the service of the Lord, because both will leave each other early in the morning'

(5b) *Si issirent dou chastel et se departirent maintenant li uns de l'autre einsi come il l'avoient porparlé, et se mistrent en la forest li uns ça et li autres la* (*Queste ...*; p. 26; ARTFL) 'They got out of the castle and then left each other as had been agreed; afterwards, they took their route towards the forest, one by this way; the other by that way'

(5c) ... *ne les diz piez ne les genouz ne se dessevroient l'un de l'autre, ne ne li estoit miex en nule partie de son cors* (Guillaume de Saint-Pathus, *Miracles de saint Louis*; p. 121; c. 1300; ARTFL) '... neither the aforementioned feet and knees got apart, nor did he feel better in whatever part of his body'

(5d) *Lancelos dit a Hestor qu'il se tese atant, quar assez en avoit dit, et il si fet; et se partent maintenant li un des autres et viennent a leur chevax et montent* (Anonymous, *Mort le roi Artu*; p. 192 ; c. 1230; ARTFL) 'Lancelot says to Hector to be quiet because too much has been said and Hector obeys ; at that moment, they leave each other, go to their horses and mount'

According to M. Manoliu (2011: 521–524), combinations of reflexive pronouns with verbs belonging to this lexical class are quite common as early as in classical Latin (*se mouere* 'quit, leave'). In her opinion, such constructions have the effect of emphasizing the very action signified by a verbal form instead of foregrounding the subject argument. Moreover, some of these pronominal constructions are allowed on a par with bare (i.e. unaccompanied by a pronoun) verbs of movement. Yet, a slight semantic difference between the two variants can be easily noted. P. Flobert (1975: 387) stresses the fact that, unlike their simple counterparts, pronominal verbs in Latin were dedicated to express the idea of a movement being performed of one's own volition. Thus, *se mouit ex urbe* would have meant 'He left the city', whereas *mouit ex urbe* could mean 'He left the city' or 'He was expulsed from the city'.

A more in-depth explanation, but which is not inconsistent with the findings of Flobert, of why various markers come to be used jointly relies on another semantic property of *se partir, se dessevrer, se departir* in the above examples. All of these verbs are inherent reciprocal (or, symmetric) predicates (see Dimitriadis 2008: 376–381 for their comprehensive semantic and syntactic characterization). In fact, getting separated relates two (groups of) individuals in such a manner that if A gets separated from B, B gets separated from A, accordingly. Given that reciprocity is already inherent in the very meaning of *se partir, se dessevrer, se departir*, additional markers can be dispensed with. Yet, *l'un l'autre* does appear. The hypothesis is, thus, that what this sequence actually does in 5a–d, is not express that some individuals happen to stand in a mutual relation to each other. Rather, its role is to highlight that this relation applies inside the set of previously identified individuals (set-internal reading; e.g. *Lancelos* and *Hestor* in 5d). An alternative, set-external interpretation, where the participants (collectively or each of them separately) stand in a reciprocal relation to an outer entity, not included in the original set, is definitely ruled out (Renaud 2002: 100–103; Haspelmath, 2007: 2105–2106). Set-internal readings go hand in hand with the syntactic completeness of a given sentence: all argument slots are filled. On the contrary, if the intended meaning implies relations with external participants ('Lancelos and Hestor, acting collectively, got separated from someone else', eligible if *l'un l'autre* is missing), it might well be the case that one of the arguments was dropped[11].

---

11 Even more frequently than by means of *l'un l'autre*, the task of discriminating set-external vs. set-internal readings is carried out, both in old and modern Romance languages, by the marker originating from the Latin prepositional phrase *inter se*. For example, the analysis of the pairs of Portuguese and Spanish sentences with and without it (a) Pt. *O chefe do clã fez os membros da família casarem-se entre si* 'The boss of the clan made family members marry with each other'; Sp. *Las esponjas y los mejillones compiten entre sí por el alimento* 'Sponges and mussels struggle against each other for

Yet, in the course of time the accumulation of the two markers ceases to be an exclusive privilege of sentences built on inherent reciprocal predicates, let alone on verbs of movement. In order to account for how the erstwhile reflexive pronoun gains new semantic function, the idea of 'bridging contexts' has been worked up by the representatives of grammaticalization theory. By and large, this explanatory tool revives the traditional perspective on relationships between reflexive and reciprocal, with the former being the source meaning and the latter – the putative semantic target. Indeed, a process going in the opposite direction has never been reported and seems unlikely to happen (Heine & Narrog, 2009: 416). Consonant with this line of reasoning is the concept of reciprocity construed as the sameness of roles played by a sufficient proportion of couples or n-tuples of participants. Put differently, if semantic roles apply interchangeably to at least two NP referents (defined on the basis of their agenthood), the relation is reciprocal (Creissels, 2006 : 17).

Depending on the functional domain that is to be dealt with, the diagram consists of either three or four overlapping phases forming a chain (initial, bridging, switch and conventionalized, with the second and the third of them being sometimes subsumed under a single one). Each of the phases surfaces as a contextually defined variant in the synchronic form of a language. At the first stage, no contextual factors constrain semantic and formal freedom of an item. The bridging phase is under way only after a given linguistic sign appears in some previously unavailable setting: aside from the source meaning, a novel semantic value becomes activated and foregrounded. The source-meaning remains eligible, which warrants the usefulness of additional markers likely to disambiguate the intended semantic value. Another phase, the shift, is equated with a series of contexts implying the deletion of a source meaning. Finally, in the last phase, the new semantic value is definitely entrenched, i.e. regularly associated with a given sequence rather than simply inferred in a restricted set of contexts. The target meaning becomes the only one available (Heine & Song, 2011: 621–623). By contrast, except for formulaic expressions, the source meaning is neither contextually

---

food' and (b) Pt. *O chefe do clã fez os membros da família casarem-se* (possibly a series of clan-external marriages is involved); Sp. *Las esponjas y los mejillones compiten por el alimento* (possibly with other living organisms) demonstrates that *entre si* is at odds with set-external readings. Moreover, this function seems to be most prominent in the case of the descendants of *inter se*, but not in the case of the descendants of *unus alterum*. Of course, a more thorough corpus-based analysis is called for to substantiate this expectation.

nor otherwise available any longer. It can survive only in archaic constructions or frozen formulae (having been superseded by *plus, magis* 'more' is found in French either as an adversative conjunction, or with its original meaning reduced to *nen pouvoir mais* 'be really fed up'; old existential *ha* is robust in present-day Spanish, but predominantly in juridical discourse, in a fixed formula: *no ha lugar a su pregunta* 'there is no place for your question', etc.).

FIG. 3.1 *A model of context-induced emergence of the* REF-REC *category*

Stage	Context	Resulting meaning
I initial	unconstrained	source meaning
II bridging context	particular syntactic environment context triggering a new meaning	target meaning foregrounded
III switch context	(set of) context(s) incompatible with the source meaning	source meaning backgrounded
IV conventionalization	the target meaning no longer needs to be supported by the context that gave rise to it	target meaning only

As far as the reflexive > reciprocal drift is concerned (conventionalizing the so-called 'REF-REC category', which accounts for all cases where the two meanings under discussion share at least one marker), the following stages have been singled out by Heine & Miyashita (2008 : 188–189): a) with singular antecedents, the element is assumed to express reflexivity only (I); b) with multiple antecedents (e.g. plural or conjoined subjects), it becomes ambiguous, expressing either reflexivity or reciprocity (=I/II). With each attestation of a newly coined $se\ V_{plur}$ pattern, speakers take advantage of analogical reasoning to entrench its innovative, i.e. reciprocal value; c) with multiple antecedents of certain verbs (e.g. inherent reciprocal predicates like *se*-verbs of movement in 5a–d above), the category expresses reciprocity only (II). Importantly, in the bridging phase, on account of the conceptual proximity between reflexivity and reciprocity, no categorical boundary sets the two readings apart. It comes as no surprise, then, that the same syntactic pattern is associated with both functional domains.

This analytical proposal does not go unimpeded. First of all, it remains dubious whether it corresponds to any chronologically circumscribed grammatical reality. In fact, no language where a specialized reflexive marker combines exclusively with singular antecedents is reported in the literature. It seems that even predicates denoting activities that are naturally performed by individuals on themselves (inherent reflexives) are not precluded beforehand from having numerous or complex antecedents[12]. In a nutshell, activities denoted by combinations such as: *se baigner* 'to have a bath', *se raser* 'to shave', *se moucher* 'to blow one's nose', *se ronger les ongles* 'to gnaw at one's fingernails', etc. can become object of serial predications as well. Such predicates are given the following definition by Faltz (1977: 3–4): 'a two-argument predication, the argument being a human agent or experiencer on the one hand and a patient on the other'. The status of the parts of 'human experiencer' is uncontroversial; they are equated with the very individual (see Riegel, 1991: 140–141).

In spite of this empirical drawback, the model should not be discarded as wholly inadequate. It accounts well for some evolutionary aspects of the Old French *se* V_{plur} sequence. The bridging phase is indeed documented as early as in classical Latin. An increasing number of occurrences of the reflexive pronoun, if in company of plural antecedents (sometimes recognizable due to the inflectional form of the verb; see Pieroni, 2010: 400 on co-indexation phenomena in null-subject languages), are capable of receiving reciprocal interpretation (see Essay 1). Ultimately, meaning selection may hinge on lexical properties of the verb and expectations of speech-act participants. Additional markers might be needed to decide which reading should be opted for. For example, some of the Latin verbs look as if an *ipse* (see 6c–d) were likely to enhance a reciprocal, rather than reflexive reading.

---

12 This criticism goes along the lines formulated by numerous scholars harshly commenting on putative beginning stages and purported starting points of various conceptual and grammatical fields, as they are presented in works of the adherents of grammaticalization theory. To mention but two examples, syntactic subordination is sometimes assumed to have originated from more basic paratactic structures. Indeed, as far as earlier stages of human languages can be systematically explored and reconstructed, embedded syntactic constituents used to be more loosely tied to their matrices than they are at present. Yet, hypotactic links have never been convincingly demonstrated to be absent altogether at whatever time in the past. As P. le Goffic (2001: 52) puts it: 'le mythe *Au début était la phrase simple ; la phrase complexe est venue ensuite* est alors dénué de fondement : un état historique de langage qui ne connaîtrait que des phrases à une seule prédication (des propositions simples), non seulement n'est pas attesté, mais est impensable'. Much in the same vein, H. Diessel (2006 : 474) expresses his scepticism towards claims to the effect that 'all grammatical markers are diachronic innovations that evolved from content words or from other grammatical markers that previously developed from a content word'. Commenting on the development of demonstrative pronouns, he concludes that despite extensive historical research there is no empirical evidence for such an assumption in this particular functional domain.

(6a) *Haec ubi dicta dedit divosque in vota vocavit, certatim* **sese** *Rutuli exhortantur in arma* Vir. *Æen* VII, 471–472 (TLL) 'When he uttered these words and called the gods to hear his vows, the Rutulians stir one another up to arms' (PG; transl. by J. W. Mackail)

(6b) *Vis, inquit, unum vel alterum, immo plurima eius audire facta? Nam ut* **se** *ament afflictim non modo incolae verum etiam Indi vel Aethiopes utrique vel ipsi Anticthones* Apuleius, *Asinus Aureus* I, 8 (TLL) 'Then answered he, Will you hear one or two, or more of her deeds? Not only does she make that the inhabitants of the country here, but also the Indians and the Ethiopians, and also the Antictons are in love with one another' (FGB)

(6c) *Perrumpere nituntur* **seque ipsi** *adhortantur, ne tantam fortunam ex manibus dimittant* Cæs. *BG* 6, 37, 10 (TLL) 'They endeavour to force an entrance and encourage one another not to cast from their hands so valuable a prize' (PG)

(6d) *Ubi milites* **sibi ipsos** *esse impedimento vidit* Cæs. *BG* 2, 25, 1 (TLL) 'Where he perceived that his men were hard pressed against each other' (PG)

Moreover, in all fairness, it must be admitted that the schema drawn up by Heine is consonant with certain findings achieved by discourse analysis research on markedness phenomena. Pragmatic analyses show that constructions complemented with additional means (hence, marked, as English personal pronouns intensified with *self* to foreground the reflexive; cf. *He washed* – *He washed himself*) prevail if speakers reckon that an unmarked structure runs the risk of being misinterpreted, thereby failing to match their communicative intentions. As for reflexive-reciprocal interrelationships, the more a speaker expects the semantics of the verbal plural to be construed as a series consisting of separate, mutually independent actions with no roles being exchanged, the lesser the need for a specialized reflexive exponent. Conversely, if such a message is intended to encode, against all odds, a reciprocal meaning, thereby possibly contradicting the expectations of addressees, *l'un l'autre* is more likely to be added. It is in this sense that the opinion according to which marked structures express communicatively marked meanings (Levinson, 2000: 328) can be seen as adequate.

A host of occurrences of bare plural verbs (i.e. without *l'un l'autre*; see 7a–b) conveying either reflexive or reciprocal meaning is easily found in OF texts as well. Many of them are potentially ambiguous. Yet, it might well be the case that their ambiguity is merely spurious. This is to say that for an overall successful understanding of the text virtually nothing hinges on which of the two readings is selected. The story goes on irrespective of whether *se connoissent* or *se voient* in the examples below are taken to mean 'know / see each other' or 'know / see each themselves'. Thus, in certain textual settings and for certain verbs, it looks as if the evolution simply stopped at the bridging phase with no further advancement towards a conventionalization of a new semantic value. If the exact interpretation of a sequence is immaterial, cumulative reciprocal sequences (i.e. with *se* alongside *l'un l'autre*) need no longer be seen as a routinized dialogic device enabling speakers to get rid of an undesired reflexive meaning (Traugott, 2010: 18–19).

(7a) ... *ne **se connoissent** mie, dont che fu grans pitez* (*Beaudouin* ..., p. 87) '... they are not aware of each other's fortune, which is a great pity'

(7b) *Et cil an furent mout dolant Qant dedanz anfermé **se voient**, Car il cuident qu'anchanté soient* (*Lancelot ou Le Chevalier de la Charrette*, v. 2332–2334, DÉCT) 'Other people were in a deep grief for having found themselves stuck inside, thinking they fell prey to a spell'

Another variant abundantly documented in medieval French texts comprises bare *se* V_{plur} sequences where the reflexive *vs.* reciprocal distinction does play a role. Yet, notwithstanding the absence of an additional marker (*l'un l'autre* or *mêmes*), their interpretation is unproblematic. The construction is sufficiently informative and the intended meaning, either unambiguously reflexive (8a and *se lassent* in 8b) or unambiguously reciprocal (8c and *se fierent* in 8b), might easily be chosen.

(8a) *Qui cundüent lur nef amunt Reposent **sei** quar lassét sunt* (Benedeit, *Voyage de Saint-Brandan*, p. 47, v. 626–627, 12–13th centuries; ARTFL) 'Those who sail their boat upstream, take a rest because they feel weary'

(8b) *Tant **se fierent** menuemant Que mout **se lassent** et recroient* (*Érec*, v. 888–889; DÉCT) 'They strike blows on each other repeatedly so that they become tired and desist'

(8c) *Avoec les x qui **se conbatent** En sont li xvi retorné* (*Cligès*, v. 1994–1995; DÉCT) 'The remaining sixteen returned to where the ten were fighting'

Therefore, an alternative account of the co-occurrence of *se* and *l'un l'autre* in OF reciprocal constructions is going to be proposed here. A spearheading step towards the joint appearance of these markers is related to an increasing rigidity of word order (Marchello-Nizia, 1999: 40–47). The point is that in medieval texts there is an almost unrestricted number of configurations of the *l'un l'autre* sequence. Its elements can appear either adjacently or be separate. Moreover, they are likely to occupy both preverbal and postverbal slots. Moreover, syntactic objects are likely to be placed medially, i.e. between *l'un* and *l'autre*. Finally, things get even more complicated with compound verb forms, where the position of the auxiliary proves pivotal[13]. In brief, any combination, short of *l'autre ... l'un* is

---

13 As for the role of the auxiliary in *l'un l'autre* placement, a convincing piece of evidence is provided by two interrogative sentences retrieved from the *Yvain ou Le Chevalier au Lion* (1177) by Chrétien de Troyes. Both contain compound forms of *conquérir*. Whereas in one of them, the two elements are contiguous and precede *avoir*, in the other the auxiliary is inserted right in the middle of them, eventually producing a

allowed. This unbridled freedom is evidenced by the examples below, which all have been retrieved from the writings of a single author. It is worth noting that the various orderings remain insensitive to the lexical semantics of the reciprocalized verb. Not only is this positional diversity proper to verbs of saying, but it also extends over verbs of fighting and hitting and verbs of intellectual or sensory actions, to name but two groups.

(9a) … *li uns a l'autre afie et jure* (*Érec*, v. 292; DÉCT) 'They are assuring each other and take mutual vows'
(9b) *Dex ! dit l'une a l'autre, lasse !* (*Érec*, v. 5461; DÉCT) 'Goodness, they say to each other, wretches that we are'
(9c) *S'a li uns a l'autre mandé qu'a la mivoie assanbleroient* (*Cligès*, v. 3992–3993; DÉCT) 'They summoned each other to meet halfway'
(9d) *Li uns son non a l'autre dist* (*Yvain ou Le Chevalier au Lion*, v. 6330; DÉCT) 'They are telling each other their names'

With the advent of the reciprocal *se*, the diversity of models tends to shrink, eventually attaining a more homogenous state. In all of the retrieved examples where the two markers under discussion are combined, *l'un* and *l'autre* surface as two contiguous parts of a single postverbal cluster. The reason seems to be that the reciprocal *se* coerces neighbouring finite verbs into taking plural forms. As a consequence, the requirements of subject-verb agreement prevent *li uns* (MASC. SG) from appearing as a subject of a sentence with a plural verb form (and the reciprocal *se*). Accordingly, the likelihood of *l'un … l'autre* to carry on acting as if its parts were substitutes of verbal arguments decreases dramatically. The spur is, thus, given to their acquiring the role of an adverbial constituent, syntactically subordinate to the verb. Hence, the *l'un … l'autre* sequence is reanalysed as a single bipartite expression *l'un l'autre*. Its unique function has consisted in enhancing the reciprocal character of the relation ever since. It might be concluded, then, that, at least in some of the examples, the integration of two etymologically and semantically distinct linguistic signs does not really serve a properly

---

split between *l'un* and *l'autre*. Cf. *Or dites : De cui se plaindra Cil qui des cos avra le pis Quant li uns l'autre avra conquis ?* (v. 6080–6082) 'So, tell me please to whom the one who suffered the severest blow is going to complain, if they come to defeat each other?' and *Quant dui chevalier sont ansanble Venu a armes en bataille, Li quex cuidiez vos qui mialz vaille, Quant li uns a l'autre conquis ?* (v. 1696–1699) 'If two knights take up arms readying themselves for a fight, which of them do you think is going to prove more valiant, if they defeat each other?'.

semantic function. Rather than contributing to forestalling potential ambiguities regarding the intended value of the pronoun, the combination of the two expressions within a single construction is but another step towards attaining the linear uniformity of French sentences[14].

Yet, factors underlying the emergence of *se* V_{plur} *l'un l'autre* are by no means limited to relations between linguistic signs. Aside from its grammar-internal facet, the process has also a direct bearing on how verbal interaction is sometimes carried out. As shown in the preceding paragraphs, the very lexical meaning of *se*-verbs is occasionally sufficiently informative to enable addressees to keep track of the communicative intentions of the speaker. The question of why *se* is complemented with *l'un l'autre* can, then, be answered if some findings of the inferential theory of semantic change (Traugott & Dasher, 2005: 93–96) are evoked. In a nutshell, reciprocity is sometimes overrepresented because speakers try to satisfy their subjectively felt need for greater clarity of discourse. Even if *l'un l'autre* contributes poorly to the propositional content of a sentence, its presence proves to be a deliberate conversational strategy aimed at getting through to the interlocutor with more effectiveness. If the value of *se* V_{plur}, reputed for being intrinsically problematic, is clarified in advance, the course of an upcoming verbal interaction is reckoned to be more fluent. In this way, the former content item (with anaphoric scope over some elements within the preceding text) turns into a more procedural one (with scope over the very fact of *se* V_{plur} being uttered). This developmental path is known as 'subjectification' (Pérez Saldanya, 1998: 28–29). Its essence lies in that an expression, instead of conveying a clear-cut referential meaning, tends to reflect authors' attitudes towards their addressees (Nicolle, 2011 : 405–407). In spite of an apparent overabundance of information produced by the co-occurrence of *se* and *l'un l'autre*, its underlying mechanism is

---

14 Even so, the model with disjoint *l'un l'autre* acting as substitutes of verbal arguments is not definitely swept away. It does persist with the subject-verb agreement being mandatory (19th century French: *L'un anéantira nécessairement l'autre, car tout être tend au plus grand développement possible de ses forces* 'They cannot help annihilating each other; obviously, any creature tends to expand their forces as much as possible', ... Balzac, *Physiologie du mariage*, p. 1053, http://ancilla.unice.fr/). The original trait of this linear variant is to allow the replacement of *l'un* with a bound variable (Old French: **Chescuns** plaint **l'autre** plius que sei RdT 6248 'Each of them is moved to pity over the other more than over himself' ; Modern French *Aucune femme n'avouera jamais être moins bien vêtue que l'autre* – my own example 'No woman will ever admit to being dressed less well than another woman' ; cf. **Les femmes ne s'avoueront jamais être moins bien vêtues aucune que l'autre*).

consonant with Grice's maxims of relevance and quantity. By using an additional marker, speakers try to prevent themselves from being asked for further indications. The constructions *se entrebattre, se pelauder, se regarder, se toucher* (see 10a–c) with overtly expressed plural antecedents and complemented with the bipartite reciprocal sequence are conceived of here as excessively informative, thus revealing Rabelais's subjective need of to minimize the risk of disconcerting his readers.

> (10a) *Soubdain ie me advise de mes lardons, & les leur gettoys au meillieu d'entre eulx, & chiens d'aller, & se entrebattre l'ung l'aultre à belles dentz, à qui auroit le lardon. Par ce moyen me laisserent, & ie les laisse aussi se pelaudant l'ung l'aultre* ... (ATHENA, François Rabelais, *Pantagruel*, Cha. X *Comment Panurge racompte* ...; D'après l'édition princeps de 1532 ; Version html: Pierre Perroud) 'But on a sudden (...) I thought upon my lardons, and threw them into the midst of the field amongst them. Then did the dogs run, and fight with one another at fair teeth which should have the lardons. By this means they left me, and I left them also bustling with and hairing one another' (PG)
>
> (10b) *Petron estoyt en ceste opinion que feussent plusieurs* **mondes soy touchans les uns les aultres** *en figure triangulaire aequilaterale* (ATHENA, François Rabelais, *Le Quart-Livre*, Cha. LV *Comment en haulte mer Pantagruel ouyt* ...; Transcription directement d'après un micro-film de l'édition Michel Fezandat de 1552. Version html: Pierre Perroud) 'Petron was of opinion that there were several worlds that touched each other in an equilateral triangle' (PG)
>
> (10c) ... *serviteurs du deffunct tous effrayez* **se reguardoient les uns les aultres** *en silence sans mot dire de bouche* (ATHENA, François Rabelais, *Le Quart-Livre*, Cha. XXVII *Comment Pantagruel raisonne sus la dicession* ...; Transcription directement d'après un micro-film de l'édition Michel Fezandat de 1552. Version html: Pierre Perroud) '... and servants to the deceased, all dismayed, gazed on each other without uttering one word' (PG)

By contrast, example 11 below reveals, in accordance with the predictions made by Heine and Miyashita, how the bipartite marker is likely to obviate the ambiguity produced by the *se* V_{plur} construction. Only after the sequence *les unes aux autres* is added, does *se peussent confesser* become sufficient to show that reciprocity represents the intended meaning.

> (11) ... *le Pape Ian XXII passant un iour par l'abbaye de Coingnaufond, feut requis par l'Abbesse, & mères discrètes, leurs conceder un indult, moyenant lequel* **se peussent confesser les unes es aultres**, *alleguantes que les femmes de religion ont quelques petites imperfections secrètes* (ATHENA, François Rabelais, *Le Tiers-Livre*, Cha. XXXIIII *Comment les femmes ordinairement* ...; Édition Fezandat, Paris, 1552, sans remaniement. Version html: Pierre Perroud) 'Pope John XXII, passing on a day through the Abbey of Toucherome, was in all humility required and besought by the abbess and other discreet mothers of the said convent to grant them an indulgence by means whereof they might confess themselves to one another, alleging that religious women were subject to some petty secret slips and imperfections' (PG)

An important fact about French examples analysed in 10a-c and 11 is that they all date back to as late as 16th century, which is suggestive of when the *se* V_{plur} *l'un l'autre* model with verbs other than the verbs of movement actually became fixed. Its entrenchment is manifestly posterior to the emergence of analogous form-meaning pairs in other Romance languages. 13th-century Catalan examples below, retrieved from the CICA database, provide a convenient illustration.

> (12a) ... *e ploraren amdós molt fort e **demanaren-se perdó la I al altre*** Crònica [B. Desclot], Pàg. II.157, linia: 15 'They wept bitterly and begged for each other's apology'
>
> (12b) ... ***ls uns ab los atres acordaren-se*** *e parlaren a i_a part que se n'irien la major partida d'éls del Pug*. Llibre dels fets del rei en Jaume, Fol.105v, linia:8 '... they agreed with one another, the greater part of them parleying apart, that they would quit the Puig'
>
> (12c) ... *nyul temps ne fos gerra entr'él e mi, si doncs nós amdós, cors a cors, no **ns desexíem la un de l'altre*** Crònica [B. Desclot], Pàg. IV.8, linia:7 '... at no time is the war waged between him and me; so that both of us, side by side, we are not separated from each other'

Such differences in the chronology of the diffusion of the *se* V_{plur} *l'un l'autre* model are at odds with some current findings achieved in diachronic and comparative Romance linguistics. They all revolve around the so-called 'pace of grammaticalization' in Romance-speaking areas. According to some scholars (De Mulder & Lamiroy, 2012: 204–208; Carlier, De Mulder & Lamiroy, 2012: 289–291), Romance languages form a scale extending from the most grammaticalized to the most conservative, i.e. the least grammaticalized one. By and large, such gradations result in the nearly unanimous conclusion that French is to be placed at the top of the scale: it is invariably classified as being the most innovative and the shifts observed in particular segments of its grammar are assumed to have been the most radical. Now, if in line with the arguments advanced by E. Traugott (2012: 18–19), subjectification is to be viewed as one of the mechanisms triggering grammaticalization, the late entrenchment of the *se* V_{plur} *l'un l'autre* construction serving communicative, rather than referential purposes, warrants some caution when interpreting such comparative claims. Far from contradicting them outright, the present investigation simply shows that, compared to syntactic structures documented in its cognate Romance vernaculars, this particular aspect of French grammar evolved with a more moderate speed (López Izquierdo, 2014: 786–787).

3.3 *L'un l'autre* in non-specific reciprocal constructions. Co-indexation problems

Linguistic items undergoing grammaticalization are believed to have corresponded, at earlier stages of a language's history, to mutually independent snatches of conversation, hardly constrained by grammatical rules. For example, the diachronic predecessor of the English *going to* future boils down to no more than a casual encounter of the *be* auxiliary followed by the gerund of the lexical verb of movement *go* with one of the possible 'directional' prepositions *to*. Each time language speakers have to do with a combination *AB* (just as *going to*), the problem arises whether *A* depends on *B* (or, vice-versa, or both are dependent on yet another item *C*), or whether they happen to be aligned by mere coincidence. In the former scenario, the *AB* combination appears to be governed by rules of grammar. Otherwise, it represents speakers' random choice, and can be used each time they feel like doing so. In this case, the *AB* combination should be viewed as belonging to discourse rather than to grammar (Detges & Waltereit, 2011: 179–180). In this perspective, grammaticalization can easily be construed as a series of shifts moving an item from discourse to grammar, i.e. a rule-governed domain (Pinto de Lima, 2014: 19–20).

In this section, yet another case will be highlighted, with the ultimate aim to show that the increasing submission of an item to rules of grammar must not be invariably equated with its having lost its former textual freedom. The case is going to be discussed with the aid of OF timeless reciprocal constructions with non-specifically used participant NPs. Notwithstanding the fact that reiterated clusters juxtaposing two inflectional forms of the same noun in Latin are documented as late as in the Vulgate (see 13a–b), this formal pattern is not maintained in the first OF texts. Thus, non-specific reciprocity is seemingly paired with no special syntactic template. It comes as no surprise, then, that the task of conveying this special semantic variant in OF texts falls back once more on the all-encompassing exponent *l'un l'autre*. A more detailed diachronic account of how it works is going to be proposed here, with an emphasis being laid on the degree of integration of *l'un l'autre* with the remaining stretches of the text.

(13a) **ferrum ferro** *acuitur et homo exacuit faciem amici sui*, Vulg. *Num* 27, 17 (BGW - BSV) 'Iron sharpens iron, so a man sharpens the countenance of his friend' (BGW - KJV)

(13b) *tradet autem* **frater fratrem** *in mortem et pater filium et insurgent filii in parentes et morte eos adficient*, Vulg. *Mat* 10, 21 (BGW - BSV) 'Brother will hand brother over for execution, and a father his child. Children will rebel against parents and have them put to death' (BGW - KJV)

Two overarching criteria according to which various classes of bipartite reciprocal sequences are divided are the presence and the type of anaphoric links with elements scattered over the same text. The first criterion is related to specific *vs.* non-specific dichotomy. This dichotomy results from judgements formulated in terms of whether an element corresponds to a unique token of a given referent or can be replaced with any other token of the same type without affecting the interpretation ('specific readings arise when the choice of referent is presented as heavily constrained, and non-specific readings arise when the choice is presented as being relatively free'; see Leonetti, 2004: 77). In late Latin, the pronouns found in *unus alterum*, *alter alterum* and *alterutrum* are required to be co-indexed with other discourse prominent elements[15], usually common nouns. Both linguistic signs, the pronoun and its antecedent, co-refer, i.e. pick the same referent in discourse. The same does not apply to nouns found in timeless reciprocal constructions. Non-specifically used items are not eligible discourse referents. Therefore, tracking of extra-linguistic entities, topic continuity or topic decay, which are indispensable for a successful discourse interpretation, are irrelevant for them. Thus, Latin clusters consisting of two adjacent forms of the same noun need not be implicated in co-reference networks. Indeed, introducing a new concept (which is exactly what non-specific elements do) does not entail introducing a new referent (Enç, 1991: 1–4). The need for textual links is, thus, seriously reduced in Latin two-noun reciprocal sequences. Actually, the degree of their integration with the remaining stretches of the same text is minimal. That is where the second criterion – the type of anaphoric links – intervenes.

As far as Latin binominal clusters are concerned, the only type of eligible anaphoric relations is binding. R. Waltereit (2012: 10–12) summarizes the difference between the two types of cohesion – binding and co-reference – in the following way: binding is a locally restricted relation (in a syntactic sense) within a linguistic sign; by contrast, co-reference operates on discourse referents and is

---

15 In Government and Binding framework, one of the basic characteristics of pronouns (alongside 'empty items' *pro*) is the referential distance between two successive mentions of the same referent in the discourse (Schwenter, 2014: 245–246). In order to calculate this distance speakers are required to look back (or sometimes ahead) to where the pronoun's antecedent (or postcedent) happens to be placed. Further compelling criteria have been devised in terms of discourse prominence to ensure more accuracy in the selection of the appropriate antecedent amid a variety of candidates (Haegeman, 1994: 43–44). This prominent element is expected to fulfil the following requirements: (i) the distance between the occurrences of two co-referential items should not be excessively long; otherwise, the prominence runs the risk of being cancelled; (ii) overtly expressed definite NPs, frequently in topical positions, are the preferable antecedents for the pronoun; (iii) no equally prominent item with different denotation in the nearby context is allowed (its presence would result in removing the prominence of the item in question); (iv) human-denoting elements outnumber by far other referentially used items; (v) *pro* is unmarkedly used to denote prominent participants.

grammatically far less constrained than binding is. Moreover, since it is confined to syntactic constructions, binding has scope over much shorter distances than co-reference. As a result, rarely does it span neighbouring sentences, let alone remote ones. No wonder, then, that nouns in sequences such as *frater fratrem* or *ferrum ferro* are not, as a rule, anaphorically paired with elements introduced elsewhere in the same text.

Seemingly, the Old French *l'un l'autre* is not very different from its Latin forerunner in terms of the degree of its textual integration. That is why its parts have been characterized as 'substitutes of verbal arguments' throughout this chapter. Yet, a closer inspection reveals that in OF a slightly more flexible use is made of the marker under discussion. In examples (16a–e), unlike in Latin, *l'un* appears with no antecedent whatsoever.

(16a) *Nul ne se vieut de mal retraire, Ne vers Dieu tourner soy et traire: Nul ne garde mes la Dieu loy. En nul n'a loiauté ne foy, Et **un voisin l'autre** conchie; L'un sur l'autre a grant envie, L'un de l'autre la marchandise Blasme, c'est envieuse guise. Loiauté ne foy mes n'i a.* (Anonymous, *Bestiaire marial*, p. 168 ; 14th century; ARTFL) 'Nobody is willing to purify themselves from evil or to turn and direct themselves to the Lord, nobody is respectful of the divine law, neither loyalty nor faith are found in humans; and one nearby creature sullies and is extremely envious of the other, playing down each other's goods, as if led by covetousness. Loyalty and faith are definitely gone'

(16b) *Tramblerent les cités desi qu'en la raïs; Trestous li firmamens par estoit si noircis Que **li uns hom de l'autre** ne pot estre choisis, Et por ce que li cieus estoit si oscurcis Ardoient en la sale mil cierge.* (Alexandre de Paris, *Roman d'Alexandre*, branche 4 ; p. 343; 12th century; ARTFL) 'The cities and their surroundings began trembling; all the sky was growing black to the point that people became unable to recognize one another. And for the sky was so dark, a thousand of candles were lit in the hall'

(16c) *Quidoient tous li puples les deust esgarder. Dont estoit fois el siecle, creanche et loiautés: Mais puis est avarisse et luxure montés, Mavaistiés et ordure, et faillie [e]s[t] bontés; **L'uns compere** ne vieut a **l'autre** foi porter Ne li enfes al pere, tant est li maus montés!* (Anonymous, *Aiol*; p. 50 ; 13th century; ARTFL) 'All the people were obliged to respect them, whereby faith, and loyalty used to reign. Then, avarice and voluptuousness alongside malice and ignominy got the upper hand, and bounty receded; ever since one buddy disbelieves the other, so does a child towards his father, such is the flourishment of evil'

(16d) *J'en conois certes plus de mil Qui sont poieur que ne fu cil Que li dyable a cros de fer Entraïnerent en enfer. Boule et baras tant monteploie Que toz li mondes s'i aploie. Tant a partot barat et guille Que **li uns freres l'autre** guille. Chascuns vielt mais vivre de boule. Milz est vaillans cilz qui mielz boule.* (Gautier de Coinci, *Miracles de Notre-Dame* ; p. 178; ARTFL) 'I am certainly aware of more than a thousand who are worse than this one is, that the devils with iron claws took to hell. Deception and trickery are swarming to such an extent that the whole world bows to them. There is so much deceit and deception all round, that brothers deceit each other; everyone is desirous to live their lives by deceiving; the more one deceives, the more one is viewed as valiant'

(16e) *Qui l'esgardoit en mi le vis, Il sambloit bien et ert avis Qu'ele deüst les genz maingier.* **Enfanz** *fuïr et desrengier Faisoit souvent aval ces rues, Et des grans genz et des menues Haïe estoit plus qu'uns vielz viautres.* **Li un enfant crïent as autres**: « *Fuionz! fuionz!* » (Gautier de Coinci, *Miracles* ..., p. 220, 13th century; ARTFL) 'The one who took a glimpse straight at her face, was aware of the fact that she must have had the habit of devouring humans, making kids flee up the streets in derangement, that she was loathed by people of high and low rank, who hated her more than an old bloodhound. The kids shout at each other: - Let's run, let's run off her'

On the syntagmatic level, instead of being distributed over different sentences or sentential constituents, *l'un* and the common noun that would in ordinary circumstances serve as its anaphoric match form a single coherent assemblage. Eventually, a new syntactic model, *li uns* N_{sing} *l'autre*, evincing a bundle of highly original textual features, becomes part of the OF syntax. Regardless of the possible absence of the anaphoric partnership for the N_{sing} under discussion, the continuity of the plot does not fall apart. It is frequently the case that the common noun does maintain some conceptual ties to what the preceding text is all about. Even if a significant referential distance separates the medial element of the *li uns* N_{sing} *l'autre* sequence and its previously mentioned conceptual counterpart (e.g. 16e does contain *enfanz* a couple of sentences before, in 16a *voisin* can easily be traced back to *homme felon*), nothing is amiss in textual coherence.

The pattern under discussion is not entirely rigid: first, the noun can vary from one construction to another, thus keeping its paradigmatic variability (see Norde, 2012 : 74–76 for how this parameter evolves in the diachrony). Second, the predicate can either be inserted in the middle or follow the reciprocal cluster (both *l'un* N_{sing} V *l'autre* and *l'un* N_{sing} *l'autre* V are attested). Even so, a bundle of recurrent constraints can be found here as well. First, in nearly all of the retrieved examples the noun bracketed by the elements of the marker is singular, thus producing a mismatch between the number of participants and the inflectional characteristic of the NP (the plural *li un enfant* in 16e is the only exception). This property stands in stark contrast to how reiterated clusters used to be organized in Latin (the freedom in the selection of number value went as far as to allow the plural and the singular to be interwoven in a single sentence; cf. *Vir viro, armis arma conserta sunt*). Second, human-denoting nouns have primacy in nearly all attestations of the *l'un* N_{sing} *l'autre* model. The only retrieved exception, containing *chose* 'thing', is given below. Note, that *l'une chose l'autre* is related here to *beisast* ('kissed') and *fere plus* ('do more'), thus looking as if its degree of textual integration were higher than in the previously discussed examples.

(17) *Oïl, ce ne cresra ja nus qu'il la **beisast** sanz **fere plus** que **l'une chose l'autre atret*** (*Perceval*, v. 3839–3841; DÉCT) 'Indeed, nobody is going to believe that he only kissed her without going further on, as these two things entail each other'.

A reduced textual cohesion of *l'un* N$_{sing}$ *l'autre* in OF offers some clues to the evolutionary mechanisms leading to its emergence. Reciprocal markers with no antecedents owe their discursive viability to the fact that they form a single form-meaning pair with a non-specifically used NP. Therefore, the Old French model is assumed to have originated as a mixture of two Latin reciprocal constructions: timeless binominal clusters and sequences with *unus alterum*. The following table summarizes features inherited from both diachronic sources.

FIG. 3.2 *Features taken by the* l'un N$_{sing}$ l'autre *sequence from Latin* unus alterum *and two-noun reciprocal clusters*

Properties taken by *l'un* N$_{sing}$ *l'autre* after Latin binominal clusters	Properties taken by *l'un* N$_{sing}$ *l'autre* after the *unus alterum* cluster
non-specifically used noun	mandatory occurrence of the two items : *l'un* and *l'autre*
unrestricted number of participants	stylistically unbiased, thus resembling late rather than classical *unus alterum*
no temporal anchorage	reiterated sequence turned into a contrast-based one
no anaphoric links between the common noun and the remaining elements of the neighbouring text	all-encompassing marker, available for the expression of any type of reciprocity

The diachronic characteristics reported above illustrate how grammaticalization sometimes proceeds. Rather than evolving from a less constrained to a more constrained status, a given item can follow in the opposite direction. In so doing, it gains more textual freedom. Erosive shifts affecting it at some levels might, thus, happen to be counterbalanced. The emergence of the *l'un* N$_{sing}$ *l'autre* pattern in OF texts is an instance of such an eventful evolutionary drift. Compared to its Latin predecessors, it exhibits a more rigorous linear arrangement of its elements. Moreover, unlike classical binominal reiterated sequences, it is quite selective regarding the morphological number of the common noun it contains. In nearly all of its attestations, only the singular is present. At the same time, once it becomes rid of tight anaphoric links, its textual flexibility increases. In line with what has been said at the beginning of the present section, if an expression fails to be involved in intricate grammatical relations with other elements, it tends to enter fortuitous, rather than rule-governed (or grammaticalized), combinations.

Essay 3. Reiterated sequences in Old Spanish. Old layer with a new typological profile

4.1 Historical continuity or coincidence of forms?

Essay 1 shed light on diachronic processes that eventually resulted in the unification of the multitude of Latin bipartite sequences by means of a single reciprocal marker *unus alterum* at the onset of the Romance era. One of the prominent symptoms of its increasing schematicity lies in its ability to be applied indiscriminately, i.e. both with specifically and non-specifically used NPs and irrespective of the cardinality of individuals involved in a given relation. Moreover, unlike its Latin forerunner, the new marker can go as far as to cease to be involved in anaphoric links with the remaining parts of the same text, as described in Essay 2. This constructional drift is underpinned by counts of frequency: expressions originating from *unus alterum* outnumber by far any other method of expressing reciprocity documented in Old Romance texts.

It has been a long-standing finding in evolutionary linguistics that shifts of the kind outlined in Essay 2 have a gradual and incremental nature. Thus, the emergence of new contexts and meanings must not be automatically equated with a definite and abrupt decline of old constructions. For example, the English *going to*-future, covering immediate intentional states of affairs, is known to have persisted for a long time alongside its primary directional value (Eckardt, 2011: 392–393). The acquisition of a new semantic function involved a set of very specific contexts: 'along with movement as a component of meaning, the source of such futures includes an imperfective (or progressive) component and an allative component' (Bybee, Pagliuca & Perkins, 1991: 30). Thus, inferences were repeatedly drawn to the effect that announcing a motion toward a specified point implies the intention of an individual to do so and to spend necessary time doing so. No wonder that contexts likely to be given either the old or the innovative interpretation are easily found (the example below and its translation are from Traugott & Dasher, 2005: 83–4).

1. *thys unhappy sowle by the vyctoryse pompys of her enmyes was goyng to be broughte into helle for the synne and onleful lustys of her body* (approx. 1482, Monk of Evesham, p. 43) 'This unhappy soul was going to be brought into hell in the victorious procession of her enemies because of the unlawful lusts of her body'

Persistent structures, which are indicative of the extinct methods of encoding a given meaning, are said to represent diachronic layers discernible in the grammar at one of its synchronic phases. In some of the approaches, layers are conceived of as one of the hallmarks of a grammatical change, nearly always inherent to grammaticalization processes. Their nature is expounded in the following way by Hopper and Traugott (2003: 124–6):

> Within a broad functional domain, new layers are continually emerging; in the process, the older layers are not necessarily discarded, but may remain to coexist with and interact with new layers. Layering is the synchronic result of successive grammaticalization of forms which contribute to the same domain.

If the conservative construction withstands erosive shifts and fails to be eliminated from the grammar, the two models are likely to become involved in semantic competition. Without necessarily being at variance (instances of an interchangeable use are not excluded beforehand), each of them becomes associated with a different set of contexts. The recent form-meaning pair attains a more schematic status. That is to say that it becomes sanctioned with a higher number of occurrences (Gisborne & Patten, 2011: 98–100). Its generality manifests itself in the number of syntactic settings it is found in. Stylistically, novel structures are classified as unmarked, hence belonging to casual rather than to careful or sophisticated speech. Conversely, old layers evince a clear-cut semantic specialization. Their contexts, possibly defined in syntactic terms, are sparse (e.g. a certain subset of subordinate clauses, exclusive of other types, may be more reluctant to incipient changes; see Bybee, 2001: 2). Ultimately, the old construction may survive as no more than a fixed formula. Its former syntagmatic privileges are, thus, seriously undermined. Vital to the above definition is the fact that both form-meaning pairs represent the same broad functional domain. A systematic account of discursive and semantic peculiarities of layers calls, thus, for a fine-tuned analysis.

The hypothesis that is going to guide the study in this essay is that the interplay of various methods of expressing reciprocity in Old Spanish (henceforth, OS) can be couched in terms of evolutionary processes outlined in the preceding paragraph. There is no denying that the *uno a otro* sequence is in the ascendant in medieval texts, thus attaining a dominant position. Its frequency surpasses that of the remnants of other bipartite clusters. In brief, it represents a novel, more schematic layer. Even so, it fails to become ubiquitous forthwith in medieval texts. Its prevalence is restricted by an older construction that consists of two parts as well (see 2a–c). Thus, the two layers set about competing inside the functional domain of reciprocity.

(2a) *Todo **uezino dalcala que salto diere a bezino**. et firiere. peche .xxij. Morauidis si prouadol fuere como fuero es & sino salues con .vi. bezinos como fuero es.* (*FVA*, fol 55r) 'Every inhabitant of Alcalá who assaults, pillages and smashes their countryman, must pay twelve maravedí if it is proved to him, as stipulated in the fuero; otherwise, he gets acquitted under the testimony of six countrymen, as the fuero says'

(2b) *Otrosi dezimos que **hermano por hermano no pueda testimoniar** en iuyzio mientra que amos estuuieren en poder de su padre* (SP, fol 188v) 'Likewise, we declare that one brother is not allowed to testify instead of the other, as long as both are under the custody of their father'

(2c) *Sy **algun omne mouio pelea con alguno otro omne** que le non fue dado por enemigo. njn lo ouiese desafiado por desonrra que le ouiese fecho seyendo fijos dalgo* ... (LE, fol 60r) 'If any man started a quarrel with any other man who neither was known to be his foe, nor to mount a challenge against him for slander, in the event that both of them are noblemen ...'

Even a cursory observation of these examples raises some doubts. First of all, one might object that sentences dealt with here are not genuine reciprocal constructions. What they actually do is simply encode a directional relation, in which one of the participants, say B, happens to be affected by another participant A, without the reverse being true. Indeed, this interpretation might have corresponded to how the lawgiver had figured out analogous judicial cases. In such scenario, *hermano por hermano* in 2b cannot be paraphrased with the aid of a simple reciprocal construction 'Los hermanos no pueden testimonar el uno por el otro / Brothers cannot testify in each other's stead'. Yet, regardless of how the set 'brothers' is internally configured, the examples above are generic statements. Put differently, they merely entail a speculative (non-assertive) character of the state of affairs they denote. Their potential, rather than factual value, is corroborated to some extent by the recurrent use of the subjunctive mood. For such sentences to be informative, no commitment as to the very existence of brothers is required. The regulation *no pueda testimoniar* 'is not allowed to testify' extends over any pair of individuals who ever happen to stand in a brotherly relation to each other. Their roles are underspecified, so that the prohibition cannot be said to relate brother 1 to brother 2 in this exact order. Ultimately, the direction is dismissed here as an irrelevant criterion[16].

---

16 A natural corollary of this decision takes us back to the definition of reciprocal relations set forth in chapter 1. In order to tackle potential judgements efficiently, it must be slightly readjusted. The formula 'a situation with two or more participants (A, B, ...) in which the relation between A and B is the same as the relation between B and A' can be replaced with: 'a situation with two or more participants (A, B, ...) in which the relation between A and B is *or can be* the same as the relation between B and A'.

The second moot point has a more properly evolutionary significance and re- volves around putative historical links between OS sentences such as those in 2 and Latin reciprocal clusters where two inflectional forms of a single common noun are juxtaposed. The question arises whether they form a historical continu- um or rather represent a random structural coincidence. Convincing arguments in favour of an independent origin of OS reiterations come from areal and histori- cal surveys. The point is that repetitions appear cross-linguistically with a very significant frequency to encode reciprocity and are evenly distributed over nearly all parts of the globe (Maslova & Nedjalkov, 2013). Rather than being due to a fortuitous speech habit, the encounter of similar looking forms may be viewed as an ingenious syntactic device to bring complex meanings and complex forms to- gether. This method has a pictorial character and involves the following analogies: a) bipartite clusters mirror the very nature of states of affairs under discussion, esp. their predominantly twofold structure; b) the sameness of the roles transferred from one participant to the other is figuratively matched by multiple occurrence of the same lexical material; iii) the simultaneous arrangement or the sequential one (with insignificant intervals) of at least two relations of the same type is rep- resented visually by the adjacency or a nearby recurrence of the same elements in the linear structure of sentences. An iconic form-meaning correspondence is, thus, yielded. The nearly universal popularity of this method might be taken as suggestive of its spontaneous rather than historically motivated emergence in OS.

Several additional clues pointing to the lack of continuity between Latin and OS reiterations are available. Spanish constructions are dissimilar in the fol- lowing respects from the ones found in Latin: a) they are typically confined to conditional constructions. More precisely, their presence is attested mainly in *si*-clauses (conditional antecedents). In Latin no systematic links between the type of clause and the use of reiterated series are recorded; b) the dominant locus for such constructions in OS involves legal codices, which is not the case in Latin; c) medieval texts offer combinations of the singular with another singular form. By contrast, in Latin the singular and the plural are distributed roughly evenly in non-specific reciprocal constructions. In Spanish, the plural of common nouns is documented mainly in narrative parts of the codices, where matters such as a legendary descent of Spanish monarchs or their presumed kinship ties to ancient heroes are dealt with in a somewhat fanciful manner. Aside from legal texts, the nominal plural is rather peripherally scattered about historical treaties devoted to events that have a clear-cut temporal anchorage (see below 4.2.1); d) unlike in classical Latin, reiterated clusters in OS codices rely exclusively on human- denoting common nouns.

Yet, in light of some distributional properties of OS binominal sequences, an alternative hypothesis on their origin is going to be advocated here. In keeping with what the definition of layering phenomena predicts, medieval reiterations offer some quaint grammatical features. At the syntactic level, they are built either on a derived (*dessafiar* in 3a) or lexical reciprocal predicate (*barallar* in 3b). The presence of the lexemes belonging to the first of these two classes is somewhat unexpected. By default, derived reciprocal predicates are supposed to fit in with simple reciprocal constructions only. Names of participants are coordinated and tend to occupy slots within a single constituent. Rules of subject-verb agreement in Old Romance coerce, then, the verb into taking a plural form. Yet, in 3a (as well as in all clusters discussed here), the two occurrences of *fijo dalgo* are not syntactically equal (the first occurrence is subject-argument and the second – the direct object, hierarchically dominated by *enviar desafiar*). This property is viewed as reminiscent of Latin clusters, where different case forms used to indicate syntactic unequality of the the two tokens of a single nominal lexeme.

(3a) Et **sy fijo dalgo enbiare dessafiar a otro fijo dalgo**. *deuel enbiar dessafiar con otro fijo dalgo* (FC, fol 64r) 'If a nobleman sends a challenge to another nobleman, he must act through an intermediary that is also a nobleman'

(3b) **Si barallar uezino con uezino** & *el uno denostar al altro por uno destos quatro denuestos: fodidenculo sieruo çigulo traydor sil firier sobre aquesto una uez con lo que toujere en mano que non se baxe por prender alguna cosa* ... (FO, fol 1r) 'If neighbours have an argument with each other and one of them slanders the other, using one of the following four words: 'sodomite', 'servant', 'cuckold', 'traitor', if, because of that, the offended hits him once with what he happens to have in hand and does not bend to pick up something ...'

Likewise, the definition formulated by Hopper and Traugott is consonant with how OS reiterated sequences behave at the semantic level. Aside from pairing reciprocity with a weird syntax, reiterated constructions contain a series of special semantic features. They are incompatible with temporal interpretation, thus denoting situations as taking place at no specific moment or time interval. Instead, they deal with habits and general or potential truths that do not require any factual basis. In doing so, they replicate nearly to the letter semantic properties of Latin binominal clusters. As has been highlighted above, no real exchange of roles whatsoever is required. Each participant is notionally defined as being able to represent both the starting point and the endpoint of a relation, but not necessarily towards the same other individual nor on the same occasion. In brief, these archaic features are seen as weighing in favour of historical continuity between OS and Latin reciprocal sequences.

The competition between the two diachronic layers becomes obvious if semantically (potential states of affairs with no time reference) and syntactically (*si*-clauses) comparable constructions with both kinds of reciprocal markers are examined. Besides conveying timeless reciprocity by means of reiterated sequences, OS appears to rely increasingly on *uno a otro* (*el uno al otro*; see 4a–b). The presence of the new model is indicative of its attaining more and more schematic rank. Nevertheless, as far as medieval legal codices are concerned, two-noun constructions will be held to represent the default option.

> (4a) [...] *mas si el uno dellos o el marido. o la mugier antes que fuessen en uno* **diere el uno al otro alguna cosa** *de su buena* ... (FJ, fol 40v) '... but if one of them, either the husband or the wife before getting married, is given things from the other's dowry ...'
>
> (4b) [...] *sy algunos han tregua de consuno & **el uno entra en los bienes del otro**. o los labra E este en cuyos bienes labra que ha tregua con el ujene a defender le que los non labre* (LE, fol 54r) 'If any men have a common truce and one of them encroaches on another's possessions or cultivates them, and the one whose possessions are being cultivated and who has a truce with the other summons him to stop cultivating them ...'

It remains to be seen how such sentences are subsequently processed. The puzzle is solved owing to some indications detectable with ease in texts compiled from the 13th to the 15th centuries. Little by little, reiterated constructions fall prey to the contamination from the influx of the elements found in the *uno a otro* marker. The process comes about in several ways and involves different phases. The most common of them consists in attaching the determiner *otro* to the second occurrence of a human-denoting noun. Although it is primarily confined to be no more than a subordinate item, the *otro* becomes more and more fixed in this kind of constructions (see 5a–b). Furthermore, the first occurence of a common noun is frequently accompanied by the article whose form coincides with *un* (see 6a–b). At that stage, OS reiterations are in an intermediate position. The merger consists in that the elements belonging to two different constructions are brought together in a single sentence.

> (5a) *Si algun **omne libre** laga **otro omne libre**. & aquel que es lagado muere luego. el que lo mata sea penado por el omiziello.* (FJ, fol. 58v) 'If any free man injures another free man and the one who has been injured dies afterwards, the man who killed him is to be punished for homicide'
>
> (5b) *Otrossi non es par dotro [...] **omne fidalgo** que furtare a **otro fidalgo** casa fuerte. o le derribare o le quemare casas o le cortare vjnnas o arboles* ... (FB, fol. 98r) 'Likewise, an equal rank is to be denied to a nobleman who steals his manor house from another nobleman, pillages it or sets fire to his belongings, or destroys his vineyards or cuts down his trees ...'
>
> (6a) *Esto es por fuero de castiella que **si vn fijo dalgo baraia con otro fijo dalgo** et parten se dela baraia. & an treguas* ... (FC, fol 134v) 'The Fuero of Castile orders that if a

nobleman quarrels with another nobleman and they put an end to their quarrel and have a truce …'

(6b) *Esto es por fuero que* **sy vn omne uende vna heredat a otro omne** … (FC, fol 55v) 'The fuero orders that if a man sells an inheritance to another man …'

In the next phase, the two elements, *uno* and *otro*, appear at once, which results in the erasure of the second occurrence of a common noun. Former direct objects surface as no more than a simple *a(l) otro*. The old layer turns into a bipartite cluster with no multiple occurrences of the same item. Thus, the *uno a otro* becomes ubiquitous at the expense of former reiterations, eventually taking over from them. The tendency is observed both in legal codices (7a) as well as in stylistically less marked texts (cf. 7b).

(7a) *Ca por qualquier destas tres razones sobre+dichas que fueren aueriguadas* **puede el vno hermano deseredar al otro** (SP, fol 352v) 'Therefore, for any of these three aforementioned reasons, if it is proved to be the case, one of the brothers is allowed to disinherit the other'

(7b) *Otrossi en dias deste Dumualdo non osauan andar ningunos ladrones nin robadores por la tierra. que matassen omne nil fiziessen mal ninguno. nin otro* **omne ninguno que fiziesse pesar a otro** (Alfonso X, *General Estoria IV*, CE) 'In this Dumualdo's days, neither thieves and bullies capable of murdering a man or of causing him another harm dared to walk around, nor a man would bring sorrow to the other'

In the remaining parts of the present essay, theoretically-based models accounting for the persistence of archaic reciprocal structures are highlighted. Textual and grammatical settings favouring the diffusion of the old layer in medieval Spanish are going to be investigated in more detail. Once they are defined, attention will be paid to typological consequences of the nearly absolute dominance of the singular of human-denoting nouns found in OS reiterated sequences.

4.2 Diachronic shift 'from above': parameters

Unless indicated otherwise, all the examples that follow have been retrieved from texts available in the HSMS - *Hispanic Seminary of Medieval Studies. Digital Library of Old Spanish Texts. Spanish Legal Texts*. In this database, medieval manuscripts received a careful philological processing (e.g. some of the omitted parts of words have been restored, basic punctuation marks have been added) so as to be readable by large audiences. The texts for the present paper[17] were randomly

---

17 The following texts were analysed: *Siete Partidas* (Oct 1491; 772,851 word tokens; abbrev. *SP*), *Leyes del estilo* (1301–1400, Madrid: Nacional, MSS/5764; 41,207 word tokens; *LE*), *Fuero de Briviesca* (1350–1450; 73,625 word tokens; *FB*), *Fueros de Castiella*

selected, so as to encompass three centuries, owing to which the persistence of the grammatical phenomena under discussion might be tracked. Yet, the primary concern here is neither the structural shifts that affected Spanish morphosyntax, nor its regional traits. In spite of the differences in size, all the sources enumerated above are treated jointly. Likewise, regardless of the variety of themes raised in some of them (mainly in the *Siete Partidas*), they exhibit an astonishing stylistic homogeneity, at least as far as purely legal sections are concerned. Importantly, stylistic unity has a bearing on which grammatical structures are dominant. As their authors intended to put potential infringements and sanctions in correspondence, *si* conditionals are the most recurrent in these codices.

For an evolutionary perspective on OS reiterated sequences, most relevant theoretical implications stem from actualisation theory of Andersen. An instance of language change may originate either 'from below' or 'from above'. These two scenarios correspond to internally or externally motivated grammatical and lexical shifts, respectively. The widespread presence of reiterated clusters in legal codices is assumed to materialize the latter ('from above') scenario. Not only is it indicative of their scholarly, external origin, but it sheds light on how these structures could have been introduced in OS grammar. If a given language change spreads from above, innovations are typically recorded in marked contexts earlier than in corresponding unmarked ones (Andersen, 2008: 36). Medieval Spanish codices offer numerous clues to how reiterated reciprocals may have spilled over to other marked contexts first and, subsequently, to the unmarked ones. Markedness is conceived of here as a multi-faceted concept, encompassing text genre, type of grammatical structure, as well as a social register.

4.2.1 Text genres

Koch and Oesterreicher (2001: 586–588) propose that various text genres be treated as points scattered along a cline extending from the proximate to the distance pole. The latter encompasses texts devised for public communication, with unknown addressees, displaying a minimal emotional load, using rare (archaic, formulaic) structures. They are habitually associated with planned communicative acts. In distance pole texts, non-specifically used NPs generally outnumber

---

(1301–1400; 79,556 word tokens; *FC*), *Fuero de Oviedo* (1295; 5,004 word tokens; *FO*), *Fuero Juzgo* (1260–1300; 99,118 word tokens; *FJ*) *Fuero Viejo de Alcalá* (1223; 22,474 word tokens; *FVA*). The dates in curly brackets indicate Specific Production Date, i.e. the year when a manuscript, not the original text, was produced, and on the basis of which concordances in the HSMS corpus were compiled.

nouns which have their full-fledged referents. This characteristic is known to go hand in hand with the tendency to express timeless states of affairs (which, in their turn, are usually associated to present tense forms; see Thénault, 2011: 163–164). Legal codices, serving special communicative purposes, are dissimilar from everyday speech. Therefore, they will be classified as belonging to marked contexts. Indeed, they evince an important ratio of structures that belong to an elevated style and, hence, fail to be reproduced *en masse* in spontaneous communication. The very nature of legal codices consists in formulating the premises of universal deontic judgements, presented as taking place at no specific moment or time interval. No wonder that dispassionate generic statements conveyed by reiterated binominal clusters are pervasive in this kind of texts, but are not in less constrained narratives, where *uno a otro* clearly prevails. Conversely, more subjective texts forming a dramatic plot belong to the proximate pole. Their presence is usually tied with the following characteristics: intimate and spontaneous communication, known addressees, a high amount of emotions (Lindschouw, 2013: 126–127). They are usually permeated with specifically used nouns and denote states of affairs assumed to take place at a given point on the time axis.

The markedness of distance-pole texts provides the explanation of another structural feature of binominal reciprocal sequences, i.e. the disproportionate number of attestations of the singular. Semantics-inflection mismatches of this kind are conceived of as arising within non-specifically used NPs. By no means is the existence of participants in such cases presupposed. Likewise, the indication of their number becomes immaterial (Rusiecki, 1991: 364–366). In other words, legislators do not commit themselves as to whether any individuals denoted by elements with this quantificational status actually exist nor how many there are. That is why occurrences of common nouns with an inherent plural[18] defy a general tendency of legal codices to have their NPs surfacing as singulars. In studies devoted to how particular number forms are cross-linguistically mapped onto particular meanings, the singular is reported to represent the default option, i.e.

---

18 In 'inherent inflection' a given inflectional feature is chosen in compliance with the speaker's communicative intentions. Instead of being elicited by combinatorial requirements of neighbouring items, inherent features convey information arising within the element in which they are found. Conversely, 'contextual inflection' applies to inflectional forms where a particular morphological feature appears as a compulsory, syntactically-induced by-product (Booij, 1996: 2; Kibort, 2010: 68–69). Linguistic signs exhibiting contextual features convey information that originates outside of them. In old Romance languages, features found in controllers of agreement are inherent, while the ones surfacing in agreement targets and in governed items are syntactically-bound.

to be better suited to represent multiple entities than the other way round (Dryer, 2013). Generic uses are typically adduced as illustrations. This is also the case for common nouns in OS codices. By contrast, in proximate pole texts, the semantics–morphology (numerous addressees – plural NP) equilibrium is easily restored: the referential plural, i.e. corresponding to cardinalities higher than one is represented by plural forms, even in binominal reciprocal sequences (cf. 8a–b).

> (8a) … *assy commo fue entre çesar & ponpeo que eran suegro & yerno enla qual guerra los romanos* **guerreauan** *los padres contra los fijos* **hermanos contra los hermanos** *& teniendo los vnos con çesar: & los otros con ponpeo.* (SP, fol 121r) '… as it befell Cæsar and Pompey who were father-in-law and son-in-law, in whose war waged by the Romans fathers were struggling against sons, brothers against brothers; some taking sides with Cæsar and some with Pompey'
>
> (8b) … *contra ellos descendio sobre ellos del cielo vna nuue muy pequeña & de aquella salio vna escuridad tan grande que a todos ellos turbo la vista: & los cego assi que no se conoscian vnos a otros: & començaronse en si a ferir tan de rezio & en tal manera que aquel dia* **se mataron** *fijos a padres & padres a fijos &* **amigos a amigos & hermanos a hermanos***: assi que murieron matandose ellos entre si de aquella guisa mas delas dos partes* (Anonymous, *Gran conquista de Ulatramar*, CE) 'From the sky a small cloud came down against them, then sprang from it so thick the darkness that everybody's sight was hampered and it blinded them so that they were unable to recognize one another; then, a harsh struggle started among themselves in such a manner that on that day sons killed fathers and so did fathers to sons, friends killed friends and brothers killed brothers'

Importantly, the example drawn from the *Gran conquista de Ultramar* shows how the drift from marked to unmarked contexts might have proceeded. The high iconicity of polyptotic sequences expressing reciprocal relations prompted their presence in more subjective and communicatively less constrained narratives. The form-meaning pair at issue is, thus, able to report even on the deeds of well-defined individuals (specifically used nouns) and the events with a clear-cut temporal anchorage. This is how a grammatical change 'from above', which initially affects stylistically marked texts, can subsequently reach genres localized at the proximate pole. The examples below have been drawn from a legendary narrative (9a) and a biblical exegesis (9b)

> (9a) *Mas que se guardassen sobre todas las otras cosas de* **matar omne a omne**. *Et por que en todas estas razones non auie aun dios dicho prologo. & tornaremos acontar dela estoria dela biblia. como auemos començado* (Alfono X, *General Estoria*, CE) 'But, above all, people were told to refrain from killing each other. And since, for all these reasons, the Lord did not tell the prologue yet, we will resume the story of the Bible'
>
> (9b) *Et los Reys de Espanna uinieron de la fuerte sangre de los Godos. por que acaescio muchas uezes que los Reys godos* **se mataron hermano a hermano** *por esta Razon* (Alfono X, *Estoria de España II*, CE) 'And the kings of Spain came from the strong blood of the

Goths, since it happened many times among the Gothic kings that brothers killed each other for this reason'

The textually-induced prevalence of the inherent singular is not the unique possible solution. In the functional domain of non-specific reciprocity, either number value can be randomly selected with no noticeable semantic effect. The proof of this is Latin clusters juxtaposing two forms of the same noun. They are earmarked for timeless reciprocal constructions, too. Unlike in medieval codices, such sentences evince an unrestricted alternation of the singular and the plural (Nkollo & Wielgosz, 2015: 343–344).

> (10a) tradet autem *frater fratrem* in mortem et pater filium et insurgent filii in parentes et morte eos adficient, Vulg. *Mat* 10, 21 (BGW - BSV) 'Brother will hand brother over for execution, and a father his child. Children will rebel against parents and have them put to death' (BGW - KJV)
> (10b) *Vir viro, armis arma* conserta sunt Curtius Rufus, *Hist* 3, 2, 13 (TLL) '(in a phalanx), man stands close to man, weapons are joined to weapons' (HTH)

All in all, the markedness of the medieval Spanish *fueros* is assumed to result from the following set of communicative features: instead of forming a consistent plot, the regulations are publicly relevant. Furthermore, rather than being extended at once to all persons who happen to have committed a specified kind of infringement, the norm is designed to come to grips with individual cases. As a consequence, each culprit can be dealt with individually. That is why the singular of human-denoting nouns in reciprocal constructions is pervasive, while plural is poorly represented. Moreover, the identity of addressees remains immaterial; all that is needed for the text to go through successfully is the public awareness of its administrative force. It comes as no surprise that these texts are permeated with unusual constructions. In spite of their non-systemic characteristic, they were unproblematic for a restricted circle of pundits (magistrates, court officials, clerks, etc.). The large audience needed not be aware of the details of all regulations, which remained in force regardless.

4.2.2 Type of clause

Another parameter whose importance proves vital to how a given construction is transmitted relates to its structural environments. From this point of view, one of the dividing lines sets apart subordinate and main clauses (the pertinence of this criterion has been extensively debated by Schøsler & Völker, 2014: 129–130). Typically, shifts of external origin are documented in embedded clauses before being spread to the matrices. Given that they are first and foremost hosted in conditional protases, whose task is to specify a potential domain of application of universal deontic judgements, polyptotic constructions in OS codices are viewed as syntactically marked. Indeed, their presence in the apodoses (main clauses) is less frequent. By contrast, other types of syntactically marked structures with reciprocal reiterations are fairly well documented, as well. They comprise comparisons introduced by *como* (11a–b) and complement clauses embedded within an indication of authority or containing a verb of saying (*dezimos* 'we say', *mandamos* 'we order', *estabelecemos* 'we establish'; 12a–b). Needless to say, in both kinds of structure no time-reference is needed. Likewise, NPs are non-specific.

(11a) *Todo xristiano bezino. que matare. o firiere. a iudeo. atal calona peche. por el iudeo.* **como pechan.** *por bezino* **xristiano.** *a* **xristiano** (*FVA*, fol 32v) 'Every Christian inhabitant who happens to kill or wound a Jew, must pay for such offence as much as is paid by the Christian inhabitant to another Christian'

(11b) [...] *digal uerdat el otro* **commo deue decir amigo a amigo** *que non la puede sanar e de lo qui hauia dado por la heredad* (*FC*, fol 55v) '... the other must tell the truth to him, as friends are supposed to do among themselves, that he is unable to cure it and must give him the thing that was given by inheritance'

(12a) **Esto es por fuero** *de todo omne que se a de saluar por los sanctos a otro omne. deuel mandar el que a de prender el derecho jurar* (*FC*, fol 40r) 'The fuero orders that every man who happens to be under the obligation to salvage himself from another man through the intercession of the saints, must act under the order of the one who is entitled to receive the oath'

(12b) *Otrosi* **dezimos que** *hermano por hermano no pueda testimoniar en iuyzio mientra que amos estuuieren en poder de su padre* (*SP*, fol 188v) 'Likewise, we declare that one brother is not allowed to testify instead of the other, as long as both are under the custody of their father'

The subsequent evolution of grammatical structures proceeds via their diffusion from syntactically marked contexts to the unmarked ones. Reiterated constructions are, then, expected to move from subordinate to main clauses. Indeed, a closer inspection reveals that OS offers some attestations of two-noun clusters in contexts that are not subordinate to any other part of a sentence. For example, the subject NP sometimes happens to be under the scope of a universal quantification (13a–b). Sequences containing such combinations resemble *si*-clauses in that their NPs are often used as antecedents for restrictive relative clauses (cf. *que deua deuda a otro omne* 'who owes a debt to another man' in 13b)[19]. Another

---

19 The actual semantic function of many types of adverbial constructions and adjunct clauses must not be invariably equated with the presence of formal markers carrying traditional labels, such as *conditional*, *concessive*, *temporal*, etc. Rather than being discrete, the boundaries separating these constructions are fluctuating and tend to overlap.

breach of the tendency of reiterated series to appear only in marked contexts takes place in straightforward declarative sentences with bare human-denoting nouns (14a–b). No overt marking of the NP's quantifying force is present here. Thus, in accordance with the evolutionary pathways posited by Andersen (2001: 237–238), legal codices have the advantage of showing how a given form-meaning pair that is initially subject to strong syntactic constraints paves its way to other seemingly less complicated environments. Yet, it must be borne in mind that two-noun clusters eventually lost the competition with the *uno a otro* maker, thus failing to become definitely entrenched.

(13a) ***Nvllus bezino de alcala.*** *o de so termino per ninguna demandanza.* ***non responda*** *sin rencuroso* ***ad otro bezino.*** *ni a senor. ni a ninguno aportelado* (FVA, fol 18r) 'No inhabitant of Alcalá or of its surroundings must be sued in any judicial case whatsoever without plaintiff by any other inhabitant, or by any lord or by any court official'

(13b) *Esto es por fuero. de* ***todo omne que deua deuda a otro omne*** *& enferma et yaze nueue dias alechugado. & es amonestado por la yglesia aquellos deudores a quien el deue la deuda seyen en la villa en aquel tiempo que yaze enfermo …* (FC, fol 37v) 'The fuero orders that every man who happens to owe a debt to another man and is ill not being allowed up for nine days, and is admonished by the church, those creditors that he owes the debt to reside in the town while he lies down …

(14a) ***Hermano contra hermano non puede fazer demanda*** *en iuyzio sobre cosa porque resçibie-se muerte o perdimiento de mienbro o ser echado dela tierra.* (SP, fol 149r) 'Brothers are not allowed to pursue legal action against each other in the event that one of them is believed to be dead, deprived one of his members or has been evicted from the land'

(14b) *Por el debdo connosçido que aya a* ***dar uezino a uezino*** *prenda pinos jllo sagione & dialos al querelloso et non le dia plazo si non quesierit.* (FO, fol 1r) 'On account of a debt that is known of and that an inhabitant has to pay to another inhabitant, pawns can be

---

Therefore, the recognition of the exact value of a given marker is also, and perhaps primarily, dependent on contextual factors likely to bring out some of its interpretations and downplay others. Functional changes can usually be viewed as the result of entrenchment processes, whereby presupposed contents and rhetorical devices are conventionalised (i.e. reanalysed as part of the encoded, rather than inferred, meaning; see König, 1988: 156–157). The effects of such contextually-induced shifts are twofold. On the one hand, they may eventually lead to the polysemy of a given marker: an expression that is traditionally associated with one type of adjunct clause is recruited for another type ever since. On the other hand, diversely labelled constructions (like the ones listed in examples 13 and 14) can convey similar meanings. For example, epistemic conditionals (see below) can be construed as relating a cause indicated in the protasis with a consequence in the apodosis. In so doing, they draw near to causal constructions. As a result, a new functional value of the conditional conjunction can become entrenched.

subject to seizure by the court magistrate and handed over to the plaintiff or not handed, if the plaintiff does not want them'

Before proceeding to the discussion on major typological issues, some more subtle remarks on OS *si*-clauses hosting reiterated sequences are needed. First, conditional sentences are not all alike, if seen against the background of epistemic links relating the propositional content of *si*-clauses to the speaker's appraisal of extra-linguistic reality. At least three variants can be singled out: factual, counterfactual and hypothetical (Schwenter, 1999: 11–12). None of them matches exactly the characteristics of protases found in OS codices. On the one hand, conditional sentences speculate about potential situations - the legislator does not take for granted that a given reciprocal relation, specified in the *si*-clause, will ever take place. As a consequence, some protases retain a touch of hypotheticality (Hunnius, 2015: 592). On the other hand, legal regulations are designed to find consistent solutions to oft-occurring situations, to prevent imminent misbehaviours or to state how, once committed, they are to be sanctioned. Therefore, protases in such texts display some degree of factuality. The situations envisaged in them are known by experience, by hindsight or by received wisdom (Diessel, 2005: 461–463), etc[20].

Such a borderline epistemic status is corroborated to some extent by lexical and grammatical traits of conditional sentences. First, as said above, it is not infrequent that the OS *si*-clauses are embedded within *dezimos que, estabelecemos que* or *esto est por fuero de* 'By virtue of the Fuero, it is the case that if' (cf. 15a–b). Given that nominal items tend to be used non-specifically in legal texts, these introductory formulae appear to be topical elements. Not only do they state that

---

20 W. Chafe's (1995: 264) opinion 'The realis – irrealis dimension has a consistent functional basis in people's judgements concerning the degree to which their ideas accord with what they believe to be objective reality' is not going to be retained here. Rather than being used to calibrate the truth of the judgements, the realis *vs.* irrealis dichotomy performs a more discourse-oriented role (Bybee, 267–268; Squartini, 2010: 112–120). The 'irrealis' pole of the axis can be defined negatively, as being at odds with straightforward assertions. Indeed, this label is frequently evoked when illocutionary effects are produced. Thus, what injunctions and prohibitions (roughly, imperatives and negated imperatives) actually do is direct rather than express belief or disbelief in what the 'objective reality' might happen to be. Be that as it may, the strength of a statement is weakened if they are used. Bare assertion is also suspended if speakers, instead of issuing a simple declaration, take an epistemic stance, etc. Thus, the meaning-truth correspondence fails to be at issue in examples 15 and 16. Instead, they deal with how the speaker conceives of his proposition in the discourse.

sequentially (and somewhat dully) enumerated textual units deal with customary states of affairs, but their task is also to ensure some continuity of these units.

(15a) **Esto es por fuero que** *sy vn omne demanda a otro omne quel forto aztor o falcon o gauylan o otra aue de caça o podencos & los fallar los podencos o las aues & gelo prouare con omnes buennos deuel dar lo suyo* (FC, fol 69r) 'The fuero orders that if a man asks another man to lend him a hawk, a falcon or an osprey or a hound dog and fails to keep the dogs or the birds, if the loss is proved to him by righteous men, he is bound to give his own [dogs or birds] in exchange'

(15b) **Esto es por fuero de grannon que** *sy vn omne demanda a otro omne que es fiador & dize el otro que el non es fiador. deuel prouar con dos vezinos derechos. & dar la deuda que el demanda & el doblo* (FC, fol 69r) 'The fuero of Grañón orders that if a man lodges a complaint against another man alleging he is guarantor and the other denies it, the proof must be made with two righteous countrymen and the debt that is being vindicated must be paid, and twice as much'

Conversely, hypotheticality, which comes near to the meaning of 'I don't know (whether the state of affairs described in the antecedent is really the case)', is grammatically underpinned by the recurrence of the conjunctive mood (Vesterinen, 2012: 80–82 for analogous values of moods in European Portuguese; cf. 16a–b). All in all, the epistemic status of *si*-conditionals will be treated as a mixture displaying some features proper to hypotheticals and some proper to factual judgements.

(16a) *Et si el sieruo firier a otro sieruo assi como es de suso dicho. el iuyz asme segundo la laga o segundo la sennal. quanto deue pechar el sieruo. o su sennor por el* (FJ, fol 58r) 'And if the servant hurts another servant in the aforementioned way, the judge calculates, on the basis of wound or injury, how much is to paid by the servant or by his lord'

(16b) *Si uezino a uezino casa* **demandar** *dia cada uno fiador en ssessaenta sueldos que el otro que vencido fuer peche sesaenta sueldos al re.* (FO, fol 1r) 'If one inhabitant claims the right of a house of another inhabitant, he is obliged to allot sixty sueldos to each guarantor and the other, who loses the case, is obliged to pay sixty suledos to the King'

Related to the above, but obeying to a slightly different set of communicative criteria, is another trichotomy: conditional constructions are different according to what the speaker is doing in the apodosis. In other words, it means that apodoses vary according to the type of predication. In content conditionals a simple assertion about external world is produced. The protasis specifies, then, the state of affairs, be it hypothetical or taken for granted, enabling speakers to issue such an assertion. The indicative mood found in some of the apodoses may be taken to reflect formally an essentially descriptive character of a given proposition: more or less fortuitous premises are, then, put in correspondence with publicly important consequences (17a–b). In speech-act conditionals, some behavioural stance is taken towards the situation communicated in the apodosis. In the texts under discussion, usually an order is issued or a particular state of affairs is opted for, which warrants the presence of the imperative mood in the apodosis (18a–b). The protasis shows, then, why or under what circumstances a given speech act is 'felicitous'. Finally, epistemic conditionals appear if an inference, whose symptoms are outlined in the protasis, is drawn by the speaker (Schwenter, 1999: 13–15). This type is virtually not represented in legal codices. In a nutshell, *si*-sentences hosting reciprocal constructions in OS are not homogenous in this respect.

> (17a) *Esto es por fuero de Castiella que sy vn fijo dalgo baraia con otro fijo dalgo [...] Et sy alguno dellos quisiere mal fazer al otro.* **deue** *ante dessafiar & de terçer dia en adelante* **puedel** *desonrrar.* (FC, fol 64r) 'The Fuero of Castile orders that if a nobleman quarrels with another nobleman [...] And if either of them intends to cause harm to the other, he must mount a challenge first and from the third day on, he is allowed to put him to shame'
>
> (17b) *SJ fidalgo a otro fidalgo quemare o derribare casas o cortare ujnnas o arboles [...] o le feziere otro mal que non tanga en su cuerpo. maguer que non le aya ante desafiado non* **es** *por ende aleuoso.* (FB, fol 95r) 'If a nobleman sets fire to another nobleman's house or pillages it or destroys his winery, cuts down grapes or trees, or causes him other non-corporal harm, even if he had been previously sued, he is not declared treacherous for that reason'

> (18a) *Si algun omne libre. laga otro omne libre. & aquel que es lagado muere luego. El que lo mata* **sea penado** *por el omiziello.* (FJ, fol. 58v) 'If any free man injures another free man and the one who has been injured dies afterwards, the man who killed him is to be punished for homicide'
>
> (18b) *Si barallar uezino con uezino & [...] sil firier sobre aquesto una uez con lo que toujere en mano que non se baxe por prender alguna cosa & non uaya a su casa por armas con quel fiera* **logrelo** *sin calonna* (FO, fol 1r) 'If neighbours have an argument with each other [...], if [the offended] hits him because of that once with what he happens to have in hand and does not bend to pick up something and does not go home to take up arms to hit the offender with, should be exempt from paying a fine'

4.2.3 External origin

Finally, the third aspect of Andersen's theory accounting for how various structures are accommodated within a language's grammar or lexicon, focuses on their origin. The distinction is drawn between indigenous and foreign constructions. In the first case, a given innovation spreads 'from below', advancing from everyday speech to more elevated registers. Changes 'from above' follow the reverse path. Legal codices, unlike strongly individuated acts of personal communication, constitute a favourable locus for the replication of constructions from

scholarly, possibly foreign, sources. Therefore, the upsurge of binominal reciprocal sequences is construed here as an instance of externally-motivated grammatical change. The markedness of the reiterated reciprocal model consists in that it
was recruited from Latin. In addition, its transfer seems to have been carried out
on purpose, as it frequently happens with attempts at achieving the renewal of
grammar. The point is that in late Middle Ages, classical Latin boasted the status
of the language of prestige (Wright, 2013: 135–7). On the one hand, the knowledge of formal Latin writings used to be a privilege of the members of the upper
crust practicing sciences, religious rites or higher administrative functions. On
the other, this particular competence was one of the criteria to be met in order to
attain such a social status.

Contact-induced grammatical shifts are sometimes known as 'gap filling'. The
phenomenon is given the following definition: 'with the replication of a category
on the model of another language, the replica language may acquire a new category for which previously there was no or no appropriate equivalent' (Heine &
Kuteva, 2005: 124). Thus, the first step in this particular mode of transmission
of reciprocal constructions entails some special communicative needs. In the
case at issue here, lawmakers were faced with a necessity to go through with
introducing efficient legal norms. If their needs failed to be fulfilled with the aid
of indigenous resources, a convenient foreign pattern was to be called for. Latin
binominal reiterations were deemed flexible enough to meet the expectations.
Indeed, even after having been subject to some formal and semantic readjust-
ments (see section 4.1), they were likely to encode social norms with sufficient
clarity. The prerequisite for their successful implementation was the bilingualism
of the medieval elite.

4.3 Typological consequences

One of the most salient features of common nouns forming reiterated clusters
in medieval Spanish codices is the pervasiveness of singular forms. By contrast,
the plural is manifestly underrepresented. An explanation of this imbalance has
to do with the nature of legal regulations. In the Middle Ages, they used to be
massively encoded by means of conditional sentences. Insofar as they serve to
express mainly hypothetical (i.e. non asserted), non-specific judgements, conditional protases host singular forms rather than their plural counterparts. As said
in section 4.2.1, non-specificity, i.e. one of the intrinsic characteristics of judicial
texts, is frequently paired with the dominance of the singular. The significance of
the mismatches in the distribution of number values is that they shed new light
on the typological treatment of some inflectional phenomena.

The diagnosis of factors responsible for the uneven distribution under discussion can be couched in terms of two oft-quoted concepts, having typological relevance: the Animacy Hierarchy (henceforth, AH; cf. 19) and the Definiteness Hierarchy (henceforth, DH; cf. 20). The thing is that their concomitant application leads to somewhat contradictory results. The first of these theoretical artefacts accounts for how number values are patterned according to what kind of entity is denoted by particular types of linguistic signs. The closer to the left end of the scale an element is, the more likely it is to evince variation in number. In Corbett's terms (2000: 56), the diagram below means that the singular – plural distinction in a given language must affect the leftmost segments of the hierarchy. As human-denoting nouns are virtually the only nominal elements in OS reiterated clusters, an important finding is that this semantic class is precluded from varying in number. The AH suggests that animate nouns are moderately variable and their occurrences in the plural must not be dismissed outright.

(19) speaker > addressee > 3rd person > kin > **human** > animate > inanimate

A crucial hypothesis assumed to explain the dominance of the singular in OS legal codices is the existence of linkages between text genre characteristics and inflectional properties of common nouns. Admittedly, this relationship is mediated via the quantificational status of NPs. Nowadays, the fact that text characteristics and the specific vs. non-specific dichotomy are interwoven is taken for granted (Koch and Oesterreicher, 2011: 135, 148–152). Likewise, the selection of the number value is known to be sensitive to the specific vs. non-specific divide. Therefore, common nouns documented in reciprocal clusters in OS are assumed to obey a different set of constraints. Their morphological behaviour can be deduced from the Definiteness Hierarchy (see Filimonova, 2005: 79), another typologically relevant construct with a scalar character. It has been devised to account for the likelihood of certain morphosyntactic phenomena (e.g. Differential Object Marking; Schwenter, 2014: 244–248; García García, 2014) according to the quantifying force of nominal items or their readiness to serve as topics (hence the alternative label – the givenness hierarchy).

(20) Personal Pronoun > Proper Noun > Definite > Specific > **Non-Specific**

Here, its assumptions are going to be extended so that it shows how particular classes of nominal items might vary in number: the higher the position of an element on the definiteness scale is, the more likely it is to evince the regular singular–plural contrast. The DH demonstrates cogently that of all classes of nominal elements, non-specific items are the most reluctant ones to accept variation in number, with the plural being significantly disfavoured. In what follows, the mechanisms responsible for the morphology–semantics mismatches in distance-pole texts are construed as resulting from the interplay of the two hierarchies described above. Their concurrent application results in mutually exclusive predictions about inflectional behaviour of common nouns. By virtue of the criteria stated in the AH, human-denoting nouns are moderately likely (or, at least, not unlikely) to inflect for number. Yet, all of them are used non-specifically in legal codices. In compliance with what follows from the DH, their non-specific status might be not in keeping with their variation in number. What is being dealt with here is known in typological linguistics as competing motivations (Furtado da Cunha, 2001: 15–17, Croft, 2003: 64–66; Diessel, 2005: 465–466). They are posited for explanatory purposes and rely on two claims: there are at least two motivations at work (M1 and M2) and M1 and M2 are in conflict. The mechanisms underlying morphology – semantics mismatches in OS codices are assumed to be best approached in terms of a clash between the AH and the DH. Since the general desiderata formulated in them cannot be satisfactorily fulfilled at once, a solution is needed. One of the possibilities has the following structure: Apart from M1, which predicts A (e.g. items X do inflect for number) and excludes B (e.g. items X do not inflect for number), there is also M2, whereby B is predicted and A is excluded. The solution is that one of the motivations (in the case under study M2, i.e. the DH) gains the upper hand over the other (M1, i.e. the AH), and B is the only outcome left. This scenario is called override (or dominance, see Moravcsik, 2014: 3–4, 6) and explains why the plural of common nouns is missing in OS legal codices[21]. Formally:

(21) apart from M1 (AH), which predicts property A (human-denoting nouns do inflect for number) and excludes property B (human-denoting nouns do not inflect for number), there is also M2 (DH), whereby B (human-denoting nouns do not inflect for number) is predicted and A (human-denoting nouns do inflect for number) is excluded. The solution is that M1 is superseded by M2, and property B is the only result left.

---

21 Three other scenarios envisaged in the calculus outlined by Moravcsik are: separation, compromise and deadlock. Their definitions have all in common the formula: 'In addition to M1, which predicts A and excludes B, there is also M2, which predicts B and excludes A'. The first scenario takes place if the domain of application of M1 and M2 splits: each yields its own structure A and B, with each principle overriding the other in a separate domain. The conflict is settled by compromise if the content of both M1 and M2 is adjusted with a single resulting structure that is similar to but not the same as A or B. Finally, it might be the case that for want of a constructive solution, there is a stalemate: neither M1 nor M2 fits. A completely new structure, unrelated to M1 or to M2, must be invented to replace the internally-conflicted one(s).

Essay 4. When do constructions fail to become entrenched? An unsuccessful attempt in Old Portuguese

5.1 Discontinuous and simple reciprocal constructions: syntax – semantics correspondences

In a cross-linguistic perspective, reciprocal constructions are divided into two major groups according to the semantic properties of the predicate. Broadly speaking, in Romance languages, semantic distinctions in the functional domain of reciprocity are mirrored on the syntactic level by two linear and hierarchical templates. The first variant can accommodate both derived and inherent (or lexical) reciprocal predicates. It consists of slots for at least three elements: names denoting participants, the predicate and the marker. The names of participants are generally patterned as coordinate, hence syntactically equal, items within a unique NP. Otherwise, if arguments denote sufficiently similar entities, they are likely to be subsumed under a single plural item. That is what Heine means by 'multiple antecedents' in his chain-like model accounting for the emergence of REF-REC category (see Essay 2). Coordinate sequences induce arguments into being assigned the same semantic role and sharing the same syntactic relation to the predicate. If the constituent hosting them is the subject, then plural agreement on the finite verb form is obligatorily triggered. This model is known as simple reciprocal construction.

The pervasiveness of null subjects in Old Romance is likely to make this basic template undergo some changes. Yet, the solutions documented in medieval texts are flexible enough to forestall the loss of any element. This is to say that in simple reciprocal constructions, slots for all the three items mentioned are provided even if the arguments happen to be omitted. If they fail to be realized as a single plural noun or two-noun coordinate structure, then the elements found in the expression originating from *unus alterum* acquire a double role. First, they are distributed over various syntactic constituents, thus gaining the ability to replace fully-fledged verbal arguments that are present in the previous stretches of discourse. Second, since they both appear in the sentence, the burden of expressing reciprocity still falls on them. Examples 1a-b below show how *um* and *outro* work with this twofold functional status.

(1a) ... *ffazemsse outras muitas cousas em huũa sazom, de guisa que **ũas torvam as outras**, a sse nom poderem comtar nos dias que acomteçerom* Fernão Lopes, *Crónica de Dom*

83

João, parte 1, cap. XXIX, 15th century (henceforth *CDJ* 1) (CIPM) 'Lots of other things happen in one season, so that they hinder one another in such a manner that all of them cannot be counted during the days that were to come'

(1b) **Esforçavomsse huũs por comssollar os outros** *CDJ* 1, CXLVIII (CIPM) 'They took pains to console one another'

If a simple reciprocal construction is built on an inherent reciprocal predicate, the unique difference lies in the presence of the marker. The very meaning of this class of linguistic signs enables speakers to do away with additional exponents of this functional value. It does not mean that markers are definitely doomed to be absent. The reasons for their eligibility in the environment of expressions denoting symmetric relations have been discussed at some length in the essay devoted to Old French. In an extreme case, in languages that tolerate covert subjects, simple reciprocal constructions boil down to no more than a bare predicate. This extreme case is illustrated by the example below.

(2) *Achas que vão destoar [estas cores]?* 'Do you think [these colours] will clash?'

The second model, besides obeying radically divergent principles of internal organization, is also dissimilar from the previous one in that it is earmarked for inherent reciprocal predicates. As far as Romance languages are concerned, the names of participants in this structural template are scattered over two different and hierarchically unequal syntactic nodes. Whereas one of them is usually a subject-argument (if it is not omitted), the other is syntactically subordinate to the predicate. Therefore, they cannot be put in a direct correspondence. Sentences based on this model are going to be referred to as 'discontinuous reciprocal constructions'. Unlike in their simple counterparts, the marker is found in this model only exceptionally. The difference between the two types of reciprocal constructions is summarized in the following table.

FIG. 5.1 *Distribution of particular classes of predicates over linear variants of reciprocal constructions*

	Simple construction	Discontinuous construction
Lexical reciprocal	Yes	Yes
Derived reciprocal	Yes	No

Very frequently, the argument in the VP is introduced via a 'comitative' preposition corresponding to the English 'with'. Yet, it must be borne in mind that other structural solutions are available as well (e.g. the symmetric predicate is a transitive verb). Moreover, it has frequently been noted that in some Romance languages there is a formal parallelism between the shape of the preposition descending from the Latin *cum* ('with', introducing oblique NPs) and the shape of the prefix appearing in numerous expressions that denote symmetric relations (see 3a–b).

(3a) *Vestia com a maior simplicidade e o seu modo de falar **condizia com** a aparência: sóbrio, sem afectação* (João Aguiar, *O homem sem nome*, 20th century; CP) 'He used to dress with simplicity and his mode of speaking matched his appearance: sober, with no affectation'

(3b) *Em 1829, construiu a Novelty, uma locomotiva a vapor que **competiu**, sem sucesso, **com** a Rocket, de George Stephenson* (*Enciclopédia*, entrada 'John Ericsson', 20th century; CP) 'In 1829, he designed a *Novelty*, a steam locomotive, that defied, with no success, George Stephenson's *Rocket*'

Far from being restricted to reflecting the basic subordination vs. coordination dichotomy, the division into simple and discontinuous reciprocal constructions has some far-reaching semantic consequences. Not only does the 'comitative' preposition entail the involvement of at least two individuals in the same event[22], but it also marks the relation as instigated principally by one of the participants, who has more control over the course of action or more initiative than the other. The co-participant is conceptually assigned a more passive role. Thus, the two individuals or objects are related asymmetrically and hierarchically.

This semantic inequality has its morphosyntactic facet in Old Romance. Since one of the arguments in discontinuous reciprocal constructions is obligatorily demoted, it cannot contribute to determining number agreement in the verb any longer. The task of coercing the verb into taking a particular number value is an exclusive privilege of the non-comitative NP representing the main participant (Stolz, 2006: 61). Moreover, oblique NPs evince a high degree of positional variability. Unlike two coordinated items, which cannot help being immediate linear

---

22 The historical relationship between comitative and NP-coordination is claimed to originate from 'with', capable of evolving into 'and', an NP-coordination marker in subsequent phases of a language's development. The opposite path has never been reported to exist. This grammatcalization chain is found mainly outside the domain of European languages. Stassen (2000: 7–18) argues that the evolution of the comitative encoding pattern (i.e. *with*) into the coordinate alignment of NPs involves the emergence of a single constituent hosting both the 'with'-phrase and the non-comitative NP. With the passage of time, the two NPs are reanalysed as being of equal syntactic rank. Although medieval data discussed in this chapter defy the direction of this evolutionary drift, they are above all indicative of an individual performance rather than of a systemic switch.

neighbours, in discontinuous constructions, the demoted NP does not always need to be adjacent to the superordinate (subject-)NP. This syntagmatic freedom, leaving the choice between adjacency or non-adjacency, might be viewed as additionally suggestive of a more peripheral position of the co-participant. Thus, the syntactic architecture of simple and discontinuous reciprocal constructions might easily be construed as a pictorial method of mapping relations between participants onto a formal level. It has the advantage of accounting for the degree to which individuals are involved in the completion of a given state of affairs.

5.2 Model-switching and its heuristic value

The starting assumption in this section concerns the dividing line between the two structural templates. On closer examination, the line rarely happens to be transgressed in Romance languages. Hence, derived reciprocal predicates are prevented from being accommodated within discontinuous constructions. The ultimate aim of the analysis that follows is to inquire into the conditions that are likely to prompt such transgressions. Then, an attempt is going to be made to ascertain what their subsequent evolution is: do unusual reciprocal constructions become entrenched or, otherwise, fail to be maintained?

The absence of direct access to speakers' bygone competence drastically reduces the role of introspection as the ultimate validating criterion in evolutionary linguistics (Pešek, 2015: 94). The analysis of an old text is supposed to be able to make up for this obstacle. Therefore, corpus-based studies are of direct relevance to understanding mechanisms that link grammatical structures evidenced in the successive stages of the history of a given language. Yet, even if at present a huge sample of medieval Portuguese texts can be easily accessed, their global size does not exceed a minimal fraction of the real language production (oral and written) of that period. In other words, a corpus offers insights into no more than a sum of individual (or idiolectal) performances (Davies, 1997: 95–96). Now, an inescapable question is: How many individual testimonies are needed to track a transition between two synchronically circumscribed phases of a given grammatical system? Representatives of the constructionist approach assume form-meaning pairs to be learned on the basis of input; what is more, systemic changes come about via a series of individual incremental micro-steps (Goldberg, 1995: 15). Therefore, even a single instance of departure from the norm might be of interest.

Surprisingly, the puzzling question of where a starting point for the shift from grammar 1 to grammar 2 is to be sought brings together construction grammar and parameter-based models. Paradoxical as it may seem, the two theoretical stances coincide in this respect. Attention paid to individual speech production in the generative tradition relies on the assumption that gradualness in a linguistic community is somewhat of an overgeneralization. It has the disadvantage of distorting the sudden, parametric shifts in the only kind of empirically available piece of evidence, namely individual grammars (Lightfoot, 1999: 77–87). Thus, idiolectal performances are necessary both to keep language working as a successful communicative tool and to constantly renew its internal organization. Put differently, synchronic variation among individuals is a prerequisite for morphosyntactic change to come into effect in the history of a language (Company Company, 2012: 680).

The empirical material meeting the above-mentioned criteria and likely to exemplify the distribution of various classes of reciprocal predicates over different templates is the *Crónica de Dom João I*, a 15th century chronicle by Fernão Lopes. The author himself explains that in his writings the charm of words is of minor importance. By contrast, his main concern is declared to lie in the bare truth of the events he recounts. Thus, to some extent his chronicle is believed to reflect features typical of spoken language rather than of an elevated style (Araujo & Gianez, 2006: 2–3). One of the most puzzling grammatical characteristics of his narrative is the recurrent use of hybrid reciprocal structures. Some of the elements characteristic of the simple model are intermixed with what is usually found in discontinuous sequences. Lopes's chronicle contains the total of 96 occurrences of constructions, both with derived and inherent reciprocal predicates, containing the marker descending from *unus alterum*. In 17 of them non-symmetric predicates are converted by means of *hũs com outros*, i.e. a sequence containing a comitative preposition. Ordinary expressions combine, then, with one of their arguments as inherent reciprocal predicates usually do. The result is summarized in the table below. Before further details are provided, some examples might be helpful. Sentences 4a–c do not rely on inherent reciprocal predicates. By contrast, the ones in 5a–c do. Yet, both groups are astonishingly similar in how their elements are linearly arranged.

FIG. 5.2 Correspondences between classes of predicates and linear templates of reciprocal constructions in Crónica de Dom João I *by Fernão Lopes*

	Simple construction	Discontinuous construction
Lexical reciprocal	Yes	Yes
Derived reciprocal	Yes*	Yes

(4a) *E começarom de a atalhar, de guisa que sse viiam hũs com outros* CDJ 1, CLXXIV (CIPM) 'And they started obstructing it, so that they were able to see one another'

(4b) *Outros sse afficavom pedimdo escaadas pera sobir açima, pera veerem que era do Meestre; e em todo isto era ho arroido atam gramde que sse nom emtemdiam huũs com os outros, nem determinavom nehuũa cousa CDJ* 1, IX (CIPM) 'Other people were striving to find ladders and climb up to see what was happening with the Master; the throng grew so thick, then, that people were unable to grasp what they were saying to each other and eventually found out nothing'.

(4c) *As gallees hũas com outras jaziam bem jumtas, e todas tiinham os rremos varados CDJ* 1, CXXXIX (CIPM) 'The galleys were left next to each other with their oars stuck'

(5a) *E esto e outras muitas rrazoões fallarom huũs com outros, mas nehuũa terminarom de sse fazer CDJ* 1, CXXXI (CIPM) 'They debated among themselves this and many other matters, but none of them was led to a successful end'

(5b) *As gemtes que esto ouviam, sahiam aa rrua veer que cousa era; e começamdo de fallar huũs com os outros, alvoraçavomsse nas voomtades, e começavõ de tomar armas cada huũ com melhor e mais asinha podia CDJ* 1, XI (CIPM) 'Having heard that, people rushed into the streets to see what was going on; as they started talking among themselves, they kindled one another's excitement, then took up the best arms possible, each as promptly as he could'

(5c) *... ca el Rey de Purtuguall, amte destas pazes, trautava secretamente gramde liamca e amizade com aquelle Ifamte dom Fernamdo, tio del Rey e seu titor, na quoall amtre as outras cousas era casarẽ seus filhos hũs com os outros CDJ* 2, CXCVII (CIPM) '... for the King of Portugal, in anticipation of these peace treaties, held secret talks over alliance and friendship with that Infant Fernando, the uncle of the King, entrusted with the tutelage over him; one of the matters raised was to intermarry their children'

The asterisk in Fig. 5.2 is meant to draw attention to some constraints imposed upon the sentences under discussion. In examples 4a and 4b, transitive verbs *entender* 'understand' and *ver* 'see', are accompanied by the REF-REC pronoun. Moreover, both the verb and the elements of the marker are plural (no attestation of the singular *um com o outro* is available). That is how these sentences are similar to simple reciprocal constructions. Verbal plural poses here an additional problem of ascertaining the status of *huũs com outros*. Two possibilities are present: it either represents a single, yet bipartite, adverbial constituent or, alternatively, *huũs* is the subject having control over verbal number and *com outros* is an oblique NP subordinate to the verb. Example 4c with a fully-fledged nominal subject (*gallees* 'galleys') blurs the distinction; as a matter of fact, more often than not, sentences of the type discussed here do not contain an overt subject-NP. Therefore, anaphoric relations are not easy to pin down accurately, and the status of *huũs* and *outros* remains underdetermined.

Be that as it may, unlike *falar* 'speak, talk' or *casar* 'marry' in 5a–c, *ver*, *entender* and *jazer* 'lie, be in a horizontal position' are two-place non-symmetric predicates. In other textual circumstances, i.e. outside reciprocal constructions, none of their arguments is tied to them via *com*[23]. In the functional domain of reciprocity, only inherent reciprocal predicates are capable of introducing oblique NPs with this preposition. That is how examples in 4a–c are similar to discontinuous constructions. The transgression is very puzzling; all the more so because no clear-cut factors influencing *com*-marking of object-arguments can be identified. In linguistic theorizing over Ibero-Romance morphosyntax, animacy is thought to be the most prominent criterion underlying the presence of prepositional direct objects. Then, specificity alongside a range of phenomena couched in terms of discourse-analysis or pragmatics (mainly revolving around topicality and the degree of individuation; for an overview of these phenomena, see Schwenter, 2014: 240–241) are adduced to explain the instances of this unusual syntactic alignment. Yet, none of these criteria fits in with *huũs com outros* in Lopes's chronicle. The singular, reputedly given preference over the plural in the selection of prepositional object marking, is not attested at all. Specific and non-specific NPs appear indiscriminately. Likewise, both animate and non-animate referents are equally likely to surface as *huũs com outros* (see 6a–b).

(6a) *Mas o desemparar do porto, que os castelãos emtão fizerão, não foy asy leixado de ligeiro que hy primeiro não ouuese hũa gramde e forte peleja de* **muitas lamças e setas e pedradas partidas bem gradamente hũs com outros**, *em que ouue asaz de feridos e mortos CDJ* 2, LV (CIPM) 'On the point of the abandonment of the harbour, which was what the Castilians set about doing then, nothing was conquered without previously waged intense struggle where lances, arrows and stones, with many killed and injured left, were thrown among both sides'

(6b) *... e nom soomente o Meestre, mas os seus* **com os** *de Nuno Allvarez* **se abraçavom e beyjavom nas faces**, *que parecia que sse nom podiam fartar huũs dos outros CDJ* 2, CLIII

---

23 The expected solution for transitive verbs would be *um ao outro*. Although, compared to Spanish, the European Portuguese is not classified as exhibiting clear-cut Direct Object Marking phenomena, things get more complicated with the preposition accompanying *outro* in this cluster. Apart from the recurrent presence of *a* with direct objects surfacing as so-called strong personal pronouns (*Chefe, não me despeça, despeça antes a ele* 'Boss, do not fire me, you'd be better firing him' instead of *despeça-o antes*) and the increasingly exceptional model *amar a* (*amar a Deus* 'to love God'), no other systematic cases of transitive verbs being followed by the 'objeto direto preposicionado' are reported in the literature on the topic (Cunha & Cintra, 2013). As for the cluster originating from *unus alterum*, the point is that the element *um* is not always a subject in a given sentence or clause (as evidenced by the example 4c with *gallees*). Consequently, *outro* does not always stand for the direct object, either. Rather, it is frequently the case that the two elements form a single bipartite unit with a more adverbial function. Yet, even in this case they are put in correspondence with the aid of *a*.

(CIPM) 'and not only the Master, but also people of his company with those of Nuno Alvarez did hug each other and exchanged kisses on cheeks, so that both seemed to be unfulfilled leaving each other'

Even more surprisingly, particular predicates accompanied by *huũs com outros* seem to be selected at the whim of the author. No dividing line sets apart various classes of lexemes defined in terms of the semantic field they represent. For example, on alternate occasions, verbs of hitting and fighting are used either with *huũs com outros* or, failing that, *outro* is the object that another preposition (e.g. *em*) ties to the verb. Seemingly, no ordering principle can be found (see *topar* in 7a–b).

(7a) *... e nehuũ podia dizer nem mostrar cousa que lhes aproveitar podesse.* **Huũs topavom com os outros** *nom veemdo caminho nem em que logar eram, e leixavomsse estar quedos, espamtados de tam desmesurada noite CDJ* 1, CLXIV (CIPM) '... and nobody was able to say how their situation could turn out better. People were coming across one another, unaware of the lane to follow and of their whereabouts, letting themselves feel hopeless and aghast at the night growing thick'
(7b) *Des hy a noite mall azada pera tall trabalho fazia* **topar hũs nos outros** *CDJ* 2, CLX-VII (CIPM) 'Therefore, once the night fell for such deeds, it made people get muddled one against another'

5.3 Abrupt vs. gradual emergence of a new form-meaning pair

It remains to be seen what are the mechanisms underlying the emergence of such non-canonical models and how they defy major findings of evolutionary linguistics. As for the former problem, the recruitment of non-symmetric predicates for discontinuous reciprocal constructions is going to be interpreted in terms of analogical extension. Gisborne and Patten (2011: 99), discussing the flourishing of the *way*-construction in English (e.g. *The wounded soldiers limped their way across the field*; see also Meinschaefer & Kelling, 2004: 442) argue that verbs exhibiting similar semantic properties tend to be accommodated to the construction first, with verbs from more distant semantic fields being documented later. With each new occurrence of the verb that starts being associated innovatively with a given syntactic template, the speaker-hearer exploits analogical reasoning to entrench the newly coined pair.

As a matter of fact, discontinuous reciprocal constructions, as they are attested in the *Crónica de Dom João I*, aside from hosting symmetric predicates, contain numerous occurrences of verbs of physical contact, including fighting and hitting. All of them denote activities that are not intrinsically required to be exchanged among two or more individuals. One of the participants might simply be construed as affecting the other, without the reverse being true. Yet, striking blows or brandishing weapons in front of someone are often interpreted as instances of aggression likely to trigger acts of defence of the same nature. Hitting or physical contact, thus, become reanalysed as tokens making up a global event of struggle that is waged by both participants and on equal terms. Likewise, rules of social politeness induce language users into viewing welcoming rituals as consisting of subevents exchanged by both participants. Indeed, there is nothing in the lexical meaning of these verbs that prevents them from being used to denote actions carried out in return, involving the same couple of inversely ordered individuals, acting side by side.

No wonder, then, that some of these verbs go on being treated as if they denoted inherently reciprocal states of affairs. By way of consequence, their presence inside discontinuous reciprocal constructions can become conventionalized. That is how analogical extensions contribute to making a construction increasingly schematic, i.e. sanctioned by more and more instances: lexical units recruited for a given syntactic pattern exhibit sufficient semantic closeness to the lexical material it ordinarily hosts. The most obvious examples of this kind in the history of European Portuguese are *combater-se com*, and, more recently (no attestations are available in the CIPM), *bater-se com* (see 8a–d).

(8a) - *Como? disse o cavaleiro, queredes que me combata com vosco?* (*Demanda do Santo Graal*, t. 241, f. 89b, 15th century, CIPM) 'I beg your pardon?, said the knight, do you want me to fight a duel with you?'

(8b) *Dês i, se homem pecou aciint(e) ou p(er) inorância, assi o deve de dizer, e sse sse combateo com a tentaçom, ou se elle meesmo a buscou* (*Castelo Perigoso*, Livro 1, cap. 16, f. 12v, 15th century, CIPM) 'Therefore, if a man sinned either knowingly or by ignorance, he should own up to that and say whether he tried to withstand temptation or exposed himself to it'

(8c) *A sorte conduzira-os à situação que sempre tinham querido evitar. Luís de Meneses batia-se com o irmão da sua estremecida Clara, Francisco de Mendonça com o pai da sua adorada Beatriz* (Manuel Pinheiro Chagas, *A Mantilha de Beatriz*, 19th century, CP) 'A stroke of fortune put them in a situation they had always wanted to avoid. Luís de Meneses came to blows with the brother of his beloved Clara, Francisco de Mendonça – with the father of his dearest Beatriz'

(8d) - *Nós temos os melhores carros e pilotos. França ou Espanha estarão atrás. Podemos bater-nos com todos eles.* (Santinho Mendes, 97 Nov 17, CP) 'It is we who have the best engines and pilots. France and Spain will stay way behind. We are able to stand up to all of them'

Our hypothesis about the origin of derived predicates occurring in the company of *huũs com os outros* relies, then, on the definition of reciprocal constructions put forward in the introductory chapter. Its essence boils down to the involvement of at least two different participants, A and B, and to the fact that the relation in which A stands to B is the same as the relation in which B stands to A. These two prerequisites remain valid both for inherent and derived reciprocal predicates. Given this common ground, the same syntactic template can be expected to tend to be applied to the two classes of linguistic signs. Regardless of the semantic features that make inherent and derived reciprocal predicates distinct, discontinuous constructions in Lopes's chronicle look as if similarities between these two classes outweighed their peculiar characteristics. That is how they come to be subsumed under a single all-encompassing pattern.

The next question relates to the longevity of such unusual form-meaning correspondences. Compared to verbs of hitting and fighting, the remaining classes of lexemes occurring with *hūs com outros* in the chronicle by Lopes fail to be maintained. In the subsequent stages of the history of European Portuguese, their semantic affinity to inherent reciprocal predicates proves insufficient to make them survive in discontinuous constructions. Although attestations of sentences like 4a–c are occasionally found in other texts drawn up in the Middle Ages (see 9a–d, *topar* 'come across somebody', *emburulhar* 'get involved'), they fail to be convincingly documented in the following centuries. Gradually, they have died out.

(9a) ... *porque virã os mouros desejosos de pelleja, abrirão a porta da barr(ei)ra & **emburylharam-se com** elles* (*Crónica do Conde D. Pedro de Meneses*, Book 1, chapter 15, 15th century, CIPM) 'because the Moors eager to join in the battle were drawing near, they propped the gateway open and got muddled up with them'

(9b) *A este apellidar acodiram algūs a porta, e o trombeta começou de tanger, **emborilhamdo-se** ja **hūs com outros**, de guisa que ficou a porta soo e os dez foram acima do muro CDJ* 2, CLXVII (CIPM) 'Once this appeal had been launched, some of them came running to the door, and the trumpet gave first blasts, bringing muddle of one with another in such a manner that nothing except the gate was left, and the ten walked up the rampart'

(9c) ... *e indo cō ella ē meo da ponte. **topou cō** aq(ue)lla alma que tragya o feixe do t(ri)go* (*Vidas de Santos de um Manuscrito Alcobacense* 5, fol. 127v, 13–14th century, CIPM) '... and walking with her in the middle of the bridge, he came across that soul that was carrying a sheaf of wheat'

(9d) *Mas era este o momento desagradável do meu dia: às vezes, ao sair, sorrateiro, do portão da igreja, **topava** com algum condiscípulo republicano, dos que me acompanhavam em Coimbra* (Eça de Queirós, *A Reliquia*, 19th century, CP) 'This was the unpleasant moment of my day: at times, moving away imperceptibly from the church's gate, I chanced upon a schoolmate, one of those who used to hook up with me in Coimbra'

Thus, something more than a bundle of individually performed transgressions is needed for a grammatical change to become conventionalized. It looks then, as if parameter-based models succeeded in defining indispensable yet insufficient conditions for the fixation of a grammar 2 inside a given speech community. A sudden breakdown of a previous individual grammar is a necessary step. Nevertheless, in order for it to spill over the whole linguistic community, a significant number of constructs is required to appear in verbal interactions among community members (Croft, 2000, 14–28; López Serena, 2014: 731–732). Only then are individual deviations from the standard model likely to attain the status of a new form-meaning pair. Thus, the failure of Lopes's non-canonical reciprocal structures is better accommodated within the constructionist approach.

References

Adams, James N. 2003. *Bilingualism and the Latin Language*. Cambridge: Cambridge University Press.

Andersen, Henning. 2001. Actualization and the (Uni)directionality of Change. In: H. Andersen (ed.), *Actualization: Linguistic Change in Progress: Papers from a Workshop held at the 14th International Conference on Historical Linguistics (Vancouver, B. C., 14 August 1999)*, Amsterdam-Philadelphia: John Benjamins, 225–238. DOI: 10.1075/cilt.219.11and.

Andersen, Henning. 2008. Grammaticalization in a speaker-oriented theory of change. In: T. Eythórsson (ed.), *Grammatical Change and Linguistic Theory*. Amsterdam-Philadelphia: John Benjamins. 11–44. DOI: 10.1075/la.113.02and.

Araujo, Valdei Lopes de; Gianez, Bruno (2006). A emergência do discurso histórico na crônica de Fernão Lopes. *Fênix. Revista de História e Estudos Culturais* Vol. 3, Ano III, n° 2 (Abril/Maio/Junho). 1–20 Online at: http://www.revistafenix.pro.br/PDF7/08%20ARTIGO%20VALDEI%20ARAUJO.pdf.

Bakker, Stephanie J. 2009. *The Noun Phrase in Ancient Greek: A Functional Analysis of the Order and Articulation of NP Constituents in Herodotus*. Leiden: Brill.

Berger, Łukasz. 2015. (Meta)discursive uses of Latin *HEUS*. *Studia Romanica Posnaniensia* 52(5). 3–22.

Bertocchi, Alessandra; Maraldi, Mirka; Orlandini, Anna. 2010. Quantification. In: Ph. Baldi and P. Cuzzolin (eds.), *New Perspectives on Historical Latin Syntax. Volume 3: Constituent Syntax: Quantification, Numerals, Possession, Anaphora*. Berlin-New York: De Gruyter. 19–174. DOI: 10.1515/9783110215465.19.

Booij, Geert. 1996. Inherent versus contextual inflection and the split morphology hypothesis. In: G. Booij and J. van Merle (eds.), *Yearbook of Morphology 1995*. Dodrecht: Kluwer Academic Publishers. 1–16. DOI: 10.1007/978-94-017-3716-6_1.

Bres, Jacques & Labeau, Emmanuelle 2015. Venir de (+ infinitive). An immediate anteriority marker in French. *Diachronica. International Journal for Historical Linguistics* 32(4). 530–570. DOI: 10.1075/dia.32.4.03bre.

Büring, Daniel. 2005. *Binding Theory*. Cambridge: Cambridge University Press.

Bybee, Joan L. 1998. 'Irrealis' as a grammatical category. *Anthropological Linguistics* 40(2). 257–271. Stable URL: http://www.jstor.org/stable/30028628.

Bybee, Joan L. 2001. Main clauses are innovative, subordinate clauses are conservative: consequences for the nature of constructions. In: J. Bybee and

M. Noonan (eds.), *Complex sentences in grammar and discourse: Essays in honor of Sandra A. Thompson*. Amsterdam-Philadelphia: John Benjamins. 1–17. DOI: 10.1075/z.110.02byb.

Bybee, Joan L. 2009. Formal universals as emergent phenomena: the origins of structure preservation. In: J. Good (ed.), *Linguistic universals and language change*. Oxford: Oxford University Press. 108–124.

Bybee, Joan L.; Pagliuca, William; Perkins, Revere D. 1991. Back to the Future. In: E. Traugott and B. Heine (eds.), *Approaches to grammaticalization, Vol. II: Types of grammatical markers*. Amsterdam-Philadelphia: John Benjamins. 17–58. DOI: 10.1075/tsl.19.2.04byb.

Bybee, Joan, Perkins, Revere; William Pagliuca. 1994. *The Evolution of Grammar: Tense, Aspect, and Modality in the languages of the world*. Chicago: University of Chicago Press.

Carlier, Anne; De Mulder, Walter; Lamiroy, Béatrice. 2012. Introduction: The pace of grammaticalization in a typological perspective. *Folia Linguistica* 46(2). 287–302. DOI: 10.1515/flin.2012.010.

Carlier, Anne. 2013. Grammaticalization in Progress in Old French: Indefinite Articles. In: D.L. Arteaga (ed.), *Research on Old French: The State of the Art*. Dodrecht: Springer. 45–60. DOI: 10.1007/978-94-007-4768-5_3.

Chafe, Wallace. 1995. The Realis-Irrealis Distinction in Caddo, the Northern Iroquoian Languages, and English. In: J.L. Bybee and S. Fleischman (eds.), *Modality in Grammar and Discourse*. Amsterdam-Philadelphia: John Benjamins. 349–365. DOI: 10.1075/tsl.32.15cha.

Company Company, Concepción. 2012. Historical Morphosyntax and Grammaticalization, In: J.I. Hualde, A. Olarrea and E. O'Rourke (eds.), *The Handbook of Hispanic Linguistics*. Oxford-Malden: Wiley-Blackwell Publishing, 673–692.

Cravens, Thomas. 2002. *Comparative Historical Dialectology. Italo-Romance clues to Ibero-Romance sound change*. Amsterdam-Philadelphia: John Benjamins. DOI: http://dx.doi.org/10.1075/cilt.231.

Creissels, Denis. 2006. *Syntaxe générale, une introduction typologique*. Vol. 2 : *La phrase : Valence verbale, transitivité et voix*. Paris: Hermes Sciences Lavoisier.

Croft, William. 2000. *Explaining language change: an evolutionary approach*. Harlow: Pearsow Education.

Croft, William. 2001. *Radical Construction Grammar. Syntactic theory in typological perspective*. Oxford: Oxford University Press.

Croft, William. 2003. *Typology and Universals* (2nd edition). Cambridge: Cambridge University Press.

Cruden, Alexander. 1835. *A Complete Concordance to the Holy Scriptures of the Old and New Testament*. Philadelphia: Thomas Wardle.

Cunha, Celso; Cintra, Lindley. 2013. *Nova gramática do português contemporáneo* (6ª edição). Lisboa: Lexikon Editorial.

Dalrymple, Mary; Kanazawa, Makoto; Kim, Yookyung; Mchombo, Sam; Peters, Stanley. 1998. Reciprocal Expressions and the Concept of Reciprocity. *Linguistics and Philosophy* 21(2). 159–210. DOI: 10.1023/A:1005330227480.

Davies, Marc. 1997. A Corpus-based Approach to Diachronic Clitic Climbing in Portuguese. *Hispanic Journal* 17. 93–111.

De Mulder, Walter; Lamiroy, Béatrice. 2012. Gradualness of grammaticalization in romance : the position of French, Spanish and Italian, In: K. Davidse, T. Breban, L. Brems and T. Mortelmans (eds.), *Grammaticalization and Language Change: New reflections*. Amsterdam-Philadelphia: John Benjamins. 199–226. DOI: 10.1075/slcs.130.08mul.

Detges, Ulrich; Waltereit, Richard. 2011. Turn-taking as a trigger for language change In: S. Dessì Schmid, U. Detges, P. Gévaudan, W. Mihatsch and R. Waltereit (eds.), *Rahmen des Sprechens. Beiträge zu Valenztheorie, Varietätenlinguistik, Kognitiven und Historischen Semantik*. Tübingen: Narr. 175–190.

Diessel, Holger. 1999. The morphosyntax of demonstratives in synchrony and diachrony. *Linguistic Typology* 3(1). 1–49. DOI: 10.1515/lity.1999.3.1.1.

Diessel, Holger. 2005. Competing motivations for the ordering of main and adverbial clauses. *Linguistics* 43(3). 449–470. DOI: 10.1515/ling.2005.43.3.449.

Diessel, Holger. 2006. Demonstratives, joint attention, and the emergence of grammar. *Cognitive Linguistics* 17. 463–489. DOI: 10.1515/COG.2006.015.

Dimitriadis, Alexis. 2008. Irreducible symmetry in reciprocal constructions. In: E. König and V. Gast (eds.), *Reciprocals and Reflexives. Theoretical and Typological Explorations*. Berlin-New York: De Gruyter, 375–409. DOI: 10.1515/9783110199147.375.

Dryer, Matthew S. 2013. Coding of Nominal Plurality. In: M.S. Dryer and M. Haselmath (eds.), *The World Atlas of Language Structures Online*. Leipzig: Max Planck Institute for Evolutionary Anthropology. Online at: http://wals.info/chapter/33 (Accessed on 2016-02-01).

Eckardt, Regine. 2011. Grammaticalization and semantic change. In: B. Heine and H. Narrog (eds.), *The Oxford Handbook of Grammaticalization*. Oxford: Oxford University Press. 389–400. DOI: 10.1093/oxfordhb/9780199586783.013.0031.

Enç, Mürvet 1991. The Semantics of Specificity. *Linguistic Inquiry* 22(1). 1–25.

Faltz, Leonard M. 1977. *Reflexivization: A Study in Universal Syntax*, Berkeley: University of California (PhD Thesis).

Filimonova, Elena. 2005. The noun phrase hierarchy and relational marking: problems and counterevidence. *Linguistic Typology* 9(1). 77–113. DOI: 10.1515/lity.2005.9.1.77.

Flobert, Pierre. 1975. *Les verbes déponents latins des origines à Charlemagne.* Paris: Belles Lettres.

Fried, Mirjam. 2013. Principles of Constructional Change. In: Th. Hoffmann and G. Trousdale (eds.), *The Oxford Handbook of Construction Grammar.* Oxford: Oxford University Press. 419–437. DOI: 10.1093/oxfordhb/9780195396683.013.0023.

Furtado da Cunha, Maria A. 2001. O modelo das motivações competidoras no domínio funcional da negação. *DELTA. Documentação de Estudos em Lingüística Teórica e Aplicada* 17(1). 1–30. DOI: 10.1590/S0102-44502001000100001.

García García, Marco. 2014. *Differentielle Objektmarkierung bei unbelebten Objekten im Spanischen.* Berlin–Boston: DeGruyter.

Gisborne, Nikolas; Patten, Amanda. 2011. Construction Grammar and Grammaticalization. In: B. Heine and H. Narrog (eds.), *The Oxford Handbook of Grammaticalization.* Oxford: Oxford University Press. 92–104. DOI: 10.1093/oxfordhb/9780199586783.013.0008.

Goldberg, Adele E. 1995. *Constructions: A Construction Grammar Approach to Argument Structure.* Chicago: University of Chicago Press.

Gras, Pedro. 2011. *Gramática de Construcciones en Interacción. Propuesta de un modelo y aplicación al análisis de estructuras independientes con marcas de subordinación en español.* Barcelona: Universitat de Barcelona (Tesi doctoral), http://hdl.handle.net/2445/35049 (Accessed on 2015–10–22).

Haegeman, Liliane. 1994. *Introduction to Government and Binding Theory.* Oxford UK – Cambridge USA: Blackwell.

Harrington, K. P. 1997. *Medieval Latin* (2nd edition; revised by Joseph Pucci, with a grammatical introduction by Alison Goddard Elliott). Chicago: University of Chicago Press.

Haspelmath, Martin. 1997. *Indefinite Pronouns.* Oxford: Oxford University Press.

Haspelmath, Martin. 2007. Further remarks on reciprocal constructions, In: V.P. Nedjalkov, with the assistance of E.Š. Geniušienė and Z. Guentchéva (eds.), *Reciprocal Constructions.* Vol. 5. Amsterdam–Philadelphia: John Benjamins. 2087–2115. DOI: 10.1075/tsl.71.74has.

Heine, Bernd; Kuteva, Tania. 2002. *World Lexicon of Grammaticalization.* Cambridge: Cambridge University Press.

Heine, Bernd; Kuteva, Tania. 2005. *Language Contact and Grammatical Change.* Cambridge: Cambridge University Press.

Heine, Bernd; Miyashita, Hiroyuki. 2008. The intersection between reflexives and reciprocals: A grammaticalization perspective. In: E. König and V. Gast (eds.), *Reciprocals and Reflexives. Theoretical and Typological Explorations*. Berlin-New York : De Gruyter. 169–223. DOI: 10.1515/9783110199147.169.

Heine, Bernd; Narrog, Heiko. 2009. Grammaticalization and Linguistic Analysis. In: B. Heine and H. Narrog (eds.), *The Oxford Handbook of Linguistic Analysis*. Oxford: Oxford University Press. 401–423. DOI: 10.1093/oxfordhb/9780199544004.013.0016.

Heine, Bernd; Song, Kyung-An. 2011. On the grammaticalization of personal pronouns. *Journal of Linguistics* 47(3). 587–630. DOI: 10.1017/S0022226711000016.

Herslund, Michael. 2012. Grammaticalisation and the internal logic of the indefinite article. *Folia Linguistica* 46(2). 341–358. DOI: 10.1515/flin.2012.012.

Hopper, Paul J.; Traugott, Elisabeth C. 2003. *Grammatcalization*. Cambridge: Cambridge University Press.

Humphreys, G.; Quinlan, P. 1987. Normal and Pathological Processes in Visual Object Constancy. In: G. Humphreys and M. Riddoch (eds.), *Visual Object Processing: A Cognitive Neuropsychological Approach*. London: Lawrence Erlbaum Associates. 43–105.

Hunnius, Klaus. 2015. Sprachgeschichte und Sprachvariation. Zur Imperfektverwendung in der Protasis des französischen Bedingungssatzes. *Zeitschrift für romanische Philologie* 131(3). 587–604. DOI: 10.1515/zrp-2015-0044.

Jungbluth, Konstanze. 2004/2005. Variação do sistema deictico nas línguas românicas. *Cadernos de Linguagem e Sociedade* 7 (ed. Izabel Magalhães). 83–105.

Kay, Paul; Fillmore, Ch.J. 1999. Grammatical constructions and linguistic generalizations: the What's X doing Y? construction. *Language* 75(1): 1–33.

Kemmer, Suzanne. 1993. *The Middle Voice*. Amsterdam-Philadelphia: John Benjamins. DOI: 10.1075/tsl.23.

Kibort, Anna. 2010. Towards a typology of grammatical features. In: A. Kibort and G.G. Corbett (eds.), *Features: Perspectives on a Key Notion in Linguistics*. Oxford: Oxford University Press. 64–106.

Koch, Peter; Oesterreicher, Wulf. 2001. Langage parlé et langage écrit. In: G. Holtus, M. Metzeltin and Ch. Schmitt (eds.), *Lexikon der Romanistischen Linguistik (LRL)*. Band I/2: *Methodologie (Sprache in der Gesellschaft / Sprache und Klassifikation / Datensammlung und -verarbeitung)*. Tübingen: Max Niemeyer. 584–627.

Koch, Peter; Oesterreicher, Wulf. 2011. Die einzelsprachlichen Merkmale des gesprochenen Französisch, Italienisch und Spanisch in diachronischer und synchronischer Perspektive. In: P. Koch and W. Oesterreicher (eds.), *Gesprochene Sache in der Romania: Französisch, Italienisch, Spanisch.* Berlin – New York: De Gruyter. 135–272. DOI: 10.1515/9783110252620.135.

König, Ekkehard. 1988. Concessive Connectives and Concessive Sentences: Cross-Linguistic Regularities and Pragmatic Principles. In: J. Hawkins (ed.), *Explaining Language Universals.* Oxford: Blackwell. 145–166.

Kuryłowicz, Jerzy. 1975 [1965]. The evolution of grammatical categories. In: J. Kuryłowicz (eds.), *Esquisses Linguistiques II.* Munich : Wilhelm Fink. 38–54.

Kveraga, Kestutis; Boshyan, Jasmine; Bar, Moshe. 2007. Magnocellular Projections as the Trigger of Top-Down Facilitation in Recognition. *The Journal of Neuroscience* 27(48). 13232–13240. DOI:10.1523/JNEUROSCI.3481-07.2007.

Le Goffic, Pierre. 2001. Sur les sources et le développement de la subordination dans le langage : l'exemple de l'indo-européen. *Recherches en linguistique et psychologie cognitive* (Travaux du CIRLEP) 16. 25–56.

Ledgeway, Adam. 2011. Grammaticalization from Latin to Romance. In: B. Heine and H. Narrog (eds.), *The Oxford Handbook of Grammaticalization.* Oxford: Oxford University Press. 719–728. DOI: 10.1093/oxfordhb/9780199586783. 013.0059.

Lehmann, Christian. 1995 [1982]. *Thoughts on Grammaticalization.* Munich: Lincom. (Orig. publ. Thoughts on Grammaticalization: A Programmatic Sketch, vol. 1. Arbeiten des Kölner Universalienprojekts 48. Köln: Institut für Sprachwissenschaft der Universität zu Köln, 1982).

Lehmann, Christian. 2004. Theory and method in grammaticalization. *Zeitschrift fur germanistische Linguistik* 32(2). 152–187. DOI: 10.1515/zfgl.2004.32.2.152.

Leonetti, Manuel. 2004. Specificity and Differential Object Marking in Spanish. *Catalan Journal of Linguistics* 3. 75–114.

Levinson, Stephen C. 2000. *Presumptive Meanings. The Theory of Generalized Conversational Implicature.* Cambridge MA: The MIT Press.

Lichtenberk, Frantisek. 1985. Multiple uses of reciprocal constructions. *Australian Journal of Linguistics* 5(1). 19–41. DOI: 10.1080/07268608508599334.

Lindschouw, Jan. 2010. Grammaticalization and language comparison in the Romance mood system, In: M.G. Becker and E.-M. Remberger (eds.), *Modality and Mood in Romance. Modal interpretation, mood selection, and mood alternation.* Berlin-New York : De Gruyter, 181–208. DOI: 10.1515/9783110234343. 2.181.

Lindschouw, Jan. 2013. Evolution and Regrammation in the Mood System: Perspectives from Old, Middle, Renaissance and Modern French. In: D.L. Arteaga (ed.), *Research on Old French: The State of the Art.* Dodrecht: Springer. 123–148. DOI: 10.1007/978-94-007-4768-5_7.

Lightfoot, David (1999). *The Development of Language: Acquisition, change and evolution*. Malden, Mass.: Blackwell.

Lloyd, Paul M. 1987/1993. *Del Latín al Español. I. Fonología y mofrología históricas de la lengua española* (Versión española de Adelino Álvarez Rodríguez). Madrid: Editorial Gredos.

López Izquierdo, Marta. 2014. Sobre la distinción innovador / conservador y los modelos secuenciales en la lingüística histórica. *RILCE. Revista de Filología Hispánica* 30(3). 776–806.

López Serena, Araceli. 2014. Selección natural, excplicatión racional y cambio linguüístico: hacina una fundamentación epistemológica no evolucionista de la teoría de la gramaticalización. *RILCE Revista de Filología Hispánica* 30(3). 724–775.

Manoliu, Maria M. 2011. Pragmatic and discourse changes. In: M. Maiden, J.Ch. Smith and A. Ledgeway (eds.), *The Cambridge history of Romance languages*. Vol. 1 *Structures*. Cambridge: Cambridge University Press, 472–531. DOI: 10.1017/CHOL9780521800723.011.

Marchello-Nizia, Christiane. 1999. *Le français en diachronie. Douze siècles d'évolution*. Paris: Ophrys.

Marchello-Nizia, Christiane. 2006. Du subjectif au spatial: l'évolution des formes et du sens des démonstratifs en français. *Langue Française* 152(4). 35–64. DOI: 10.3406/lfr.2006.6639.

Martins, Ana M. 2014. Syntactic change in Portuguese and Spanish. Divergent and parallel patterns of linguistic splitting. In: P. Amaral and A.M. Carvalho (eds.), *Portuguese-Spanish Interfaces. Diachrony, synchrony, and contact*. Amsterdam-Philadelphia: John Benjamins, 237–260. DOI: 10.1075/ihll.1.04mar.

Maslova, Elena; Nedjalkov, Vladimir P. 2013. Reciprocal Constructions. In: M.S. Dryer and M. Haspelmath (eds.), *The World Atlas of Language Structures Online*. Leipzig: Mac Planck Institute for Evolutionary Anthroplogy. Online at: http://wals.info/chapter/106 (Accessed on 2015–12–31).

Matras, Yaron. 2011. Grammaticalization and language contact. In: B. Heine and H. Narrog (eds.), *The Oxford Handbook of Grammaticalization*. Oxford: Oxford University Press. 279–290. DOI: 10.1093/oxfordhb/9780199586783.013.0022.

Meillet, Antoine. 1904/1905. Comment les mots changent de sens ? *L'Année sociologique* (1896/1897–1924/1925). 1–38. Stable URL: http://www.jstor.org/stable/27882636.

Meinschaefer, Judith; Kelling, Carmen. 2004. How lexicalization patterns influence syntax: Motion verbs in French and English In: M. Andronis, E. Debenport, A. Pycha and K. Yoshimura (eds.), *Proceedings of the Chicago Linguistic Society*, Volume I of CLS 38. Chicago: University of Chicago. 437–452.

Mel'cuk, Igor. 2006. *Aspects of the Theory of Morphology*. Berlin-New York: De Gruyter. DOI : 10.1515/9783110199864.

Menge, Hermann. 1900. *Repetitorium der Lateinischen Syntax und Stilistik. Ein Lernbuch für Studierende Und Vorgeschrittene Schüler, zugleich ein praktisches Repertorium für Lehrer*. Wolfenbüttel: Julius Zwißler Verlag. https://archive.org/details/RepetitoriumDerLateinischenSyntaxUndStilistik.

Moravcsik, Edith. 2014. Introduction. In: E. Moravcsik, B. MacWhinney and A. Malchukov (eds.), *Competing Motivations in Grammar and Usage*. Oxford: Oxford University Press. 1–14.

Nicolle, Steve. 2011. Pragmatic Aspects of Grammaticalization, In: B. Heine and H. Narrog (eds.), *The Oxford Handbook of Grammaticalization*. Oxford: Oxford University Press. 401–412. DOI: 10.1093/oxfordhb/9780199586783.013.0032.

Nkollo, Mikołaj. 2013a. L'expression de la réciprocité en ancien français. Mécanismes grammaticaux et leur évolution. *Romanische Forschungen. Vierteljahrsschrift für romanische Sprachen und Literaturen* 125(1). 14–31. DOI: 10.3196/003581213805393405.

Nkollo, Mikołaj. 2013b. La réciprocité dans les langues romanes anciennes: Le français et le portugais. Scénarios de grammaticalisation. *Revue Romane. Langue et littérature. International Journal of Romance Languages and Literatures*, 48(2). 284–306. DOI: 10.1075/rro.48.2.04nko.

Nkollo, Mikołaj; Wielgosz, Małgorzata. 2015. El reciproco 'uno a otro' y sus variedades en el español medieval: Un estudio evolutivo. *Romance Philology* 68(2). 339–368. DOI: 10.1484/J.RPH.5.107641.

Norde, Muriel. 2012. Lehmann's parameters revisited. In: K. Davidse, T. Breban, L. Brems and T. Mortelmans (eds.), *Grammaticalization and Language Change. New reflections*. Amsterdam-Philadelphia: John Benjamins. 73–109. DOI: 10.1075/slcs.130.04nor.

Penny, Ralph. 2002. *A History of the Spanish Language*. Cambridge: Cambridge University Press.

Pérez Saldanya, Manuel. 1998. *Del llatí al català. Morfosintaxi verbal històrica*. València: Universitat de València.

Pešek, Ondřej. 2015. Concessive Clauses in 'Li Livres de confort de philosophie' by Jean de Meun: A case study of an idiolectal performance. *Studia Romanica Posnaniensia* 42(5). 93–112.

Pieroni, Silvia. 2010. Deixis and anaphora, In: P. Baldi and P. Cuzzolin (eds.), *New Perspectives on Historical Latin Syntax*. Vol. 3: *Constituent Syntax: Quantification, Numerals, Possession, Anaphora*. Berlin-New York: De Gruyter. 389–501. DOI: 10.1515/9783110215465.389.

Pinkster, Harm. 2015. *The Oxford Latin Syntax. Vol. 1 The Simple Clause*. Oxford: Oxford University Press.

Pinto de Lima, José. 2014. *Studies on Grammaticalization and Lexicalization – Estudos de Gramaticalização e Lexicalização*. Munich: Lincom.

Renaud, Francis. 2002. Les bases de la quantification réciproque. *Linx. Revue des linguistes de l'Université Paris Ouest Nanterre La Défense* 47 ('Du sens au sens. Hommage à Michel Galmiche'). 89–106. DOI: 10.4000/linx.586.

Riegel, Martin 1991. Transitivité et conditionnements cognitifs: la relation partie-tout et la complémentation verbale, *Linx. Revue des linguistes de l'Université Paris Ouest Nanterre La Défense* 24. 133–146.

Rusiecki, Jan. 1991. Generic sentences, classes of predicate and definite generic noun phrases. In: M. Grochowski and D. Weiss (eds.), *Words are Physicians for an Ailing Mind*. Munich: Otto Sagner. 363–370.

Schøsler, Lene; Völker, Harald. 2014. Intralinguistic and extralinguistic variation factors in Old French negation with *ne-Ø, ne-mie, ne-pas* and *ne-point* across different text types. *Journal of French Language Studies* 24(1). 127–153. DOI: 10.1017/S0959269513000379.

Schwenter, Scott A. 1999. *Pragmatics of conditional marking: implicature, scalarity and exclusivity*. New York-London: Garland Press.

Schwenter, Scott A. 2014. Two kinds of differential object marking in Portuguese and Spanish. In: P. Amaral and A.M. Carvalho (eds.), *Portuguese-Spanish Interfaces. Diachrony, synchrony, and contact*. Amsterdam-Philadelphia: John Benjamins, 237–260. DOI: 10.1075/ihll.1.12sch.

Squartini, Mario. 2010. Where mood, modality and illocution meet: the morphosyntax of Romance conjectures. In: M.G. Becker and E-M. Remberger (eds.), *Modality and Mood in Romance. Modal interpretation, mood selection and mood alternation*. Berlin-New York: De Gruyter. 109–132. DOI: 10.1515/9783110234343.1.109.

Stolz, Thomas. 2006. *On Comitatives and Related Categories. A Typological Study with Special Focus on the Languages of Europe*. Berlin-New York: De Gruyter.

Stassen, Leon. 2000. AND-languages and WITH-languages. *Linguistic Typology* 4(1). 1–54. DOI: 10.1515/lity.2000.4.1.1.

Stavinschi, Alexandra. 2012. On the development of the Romance demonstrative systems. Historical remarks and theoretical conclusions. *Diachronica. International Journal for Historical Linguistics* 29(1). 72–97. DOI: 10.1075/dia.29.1.03sta.

Tekavčič, Pavao. 1980. *Grammatica storica dell'italiano*, 2: *Morfosintassi*. Bologna: Il Mulino.

Thénault, Créola. 2011. Valeurs du présent français et genres de discours. *Linx. Revue des linguistes de l'Université Paris Ouest Nanterre La Défense* 64/65 ('Les genres de discours vus par la grammaire'). 155–172. DOI: 10.4000/linx.1410.

Traina, Alfonso; Bertotti, Tullio. 1985. *Sintassi normativa della lingua latina*. Bologna: Cappelli.

Traugott, Elisabeth C. 2008. The grammaticalization of *NP of NP* patterns. In: A. Bergs and G. Diewald (eds.), *Constructions and language change*. Berlin-New York: De Gruyter, 23–45. DOI: 10.1515/9783110211757.23.

Traugott, Elisabeth C. 2010. Dialogic Contexts as Motivations for Syntactic Change. In: R.A. Cloutier, A.M. Hamilton-Brehm and W.A Kretzschmar, Jr. (eds.), *Studies in the History of the English Language V. Variation and Change in English Grammar and Lexicon: Contemporary Approaches*. Berlin-New York: De Gruyter. 11–36. DOI: 10.1515/9783110220339.1.11.

Traugott, Elisabeth C. 2012. Intersubjectification and clause periphery. *English Text Construction* 5(1). 7–28. DOI: 10.1075/etc.5.1.02trau.

Traugott, Elisabeth C.; Dasher, Richard. 2005. *The Regularity in Semantic Change*. Cambridge: Cambridge University Press.

Trousdale, Graeme 2012. Grammaticalization, constructions and the grammaticalization of constructions. In: K. Davidse, T. Breban, L. Brems and T. Mortelmans (eds.), *Grammaticalization and Language Change: New reflections*. Amsterdam–Philadelphia: John Benjamins. 167–198. DOI: 10.1075/slcs.130.07tro.

Trousdale, Graeme 2014. On the relationship between grammaticalization and constructionalization. *Folia Linguistica* 48(2). 557–578. DOI: 10.1515/flin.2014.018.

Vesterinen, Rainer. 2012. O modo verbal em expressões impessoais com o verbo 'ser'. *Revue Romane. Langue et littérature. International Journal of Romance Languages and Literatures* 47(1). 76–97. DOI: 10.1075/rro.47.1.04ves.

Waltereit, Richard. 2012. *Reflexive Marking in the History of French*. Amsterdam–Philadelphia: John Benjamins. DOI: 10.1075/slcs.127.

Wright, Roger. 2013. A Sociophilological Study of the Change to Official Romance Documentation in Castile. In: M. Garrison, A.P. Orbán & M. Mostert (eds.), *Spoken and Written Language. Relations between Latin and the Vernacular Languages in the Earlier Middle Ages*. Brussels: Brepols. 133–147. DOI: 10.1484/M.USML-EB.5.100917.

Sources and translations

archive org. *The Comedies of Plautus*. Literally translated into English Prose, with notes by Henry Thomas Riley, M.A. Vol. II. London, G. Bell & sons, Ltd. 1913

ARTFL - TFA. The ARTFL Project. Textes de Français Ancien (TFA). Department of Romance Languages and Literatures, Division of the Humanities, University of Chicago.

- Anonymous [1150], *Roman de Thèbes* (publié par G. Raynaud de Lage, tome I, Paris, Champion, 1966).

- Wace [1155], *Partie arthurienne du Roman de Brut* (éd. par Ivor Arnold et Margaret Pelan, Paris, Klincksieck, 1962).

- Anonymous [1175], *Quatre Livres des Rois* (Li Quatre Livre des Reis, éd. par Ernst R. Curtius, Dresden-Halle, Niemeyer, 1911).

- Alexandre de Paris [1180], *Roman d' Alexandre, branche 4* (The Medieval French Roman d'Alexandre, éd. par E.C. Armstrong, D.L. Buffum).

- Benedeit [1106–1121], *Voyage de Saint-Brandan* (The Anglo-norman Voyage of St Brendan, éd. par Ian Short et Brian Merrilees).

- Anonymous [1200], *Vengeance Raguidel* (éd. par May Plouzeau, Ottawa, site LFA, 2002).

- Anonymous [1210 (?)], *Aiol* (Aiol. Chanson de geste, éd. par Jacques Normand et Gaston Raynaud, Paris, Société des)

- Gautier de Coinci [1218–1227], *Miracles de Notre-Dame* (éd. par V. Frederic Koenig, tome troisième, Genève)

- Anonymous [1225], *Queste del Saint Graal* (éd. par Albert Pauphilet, Paris, Champion, 1949).

- Guillaume de Saint-Pathus [c. 1300], *Miracles de saint Louis* (éd. par Percival B. Fay, Paris, CFMA, 1931).

- Anonymous [c. 1230], *Mort le roi Artu* (éd. par Jean Frappier, Genève, Droz, 1964).

- Anonymous [1333 (?)], *Bestiaire marial* (Le Bestiaire marial tiré du Rosarius (Paris, ms. BN fr. 12483), éd. Par Angela Mattiacci).

- Anonymous [1350], *Beaudouin de Sebourc* (éd. par Larry Crist, 2 volumes, Abbeville, SATF, 2002).

ATHENA - Pierre Perroud http://athena.unige.ch/athena/bon/bon_prefaces_rabelais.html (accès le 20 novembre 2015). D'après l'édition princeps de 1532.

BGW - Bible Gateway

- BSV. *Biblia Sacra iuxta vulgatam versionem*. Originally published in 1969 (4th edition 1994). https://www.biblegateway.com/versions/Biblia-Sacra-Vulgata-VULGATE/#booklist

- KJV. *King James Version*. Originally published in 1611 (the 1987 printing; public domain in the US) https://www.biblegateway.com/versions/King-James-Version-KJV-Bible/

CE - Davies, Mark. (2002-) *Corpus del Español: 100 million words, 1200s-1900s*. Available online at http://www.corpusdelespanol.org.

- Alfono X, *General Estoria*, Electronic Texts and Concordances of the Madison Corpus of Early Spanish Manuscripts and Printings. Prepared by John ONeill, Madison and New York, 1999. CD-ROM ISBN 1-56954-122-1. Madrid Nacional ms. 816

- Alfonso X, *General Estoria IV*, Texts and Concordances of the Madison Corpus of Early Spanish Manuscripts and Printings. Prepared by John ONeill, Madison and New York, 1999. CD-ROM ISBN 1-56954-122-1. Roma Vaticana Urb lat 539

- Alfono X, *Estoria de España II*, Electronic Texts and Concordances of the Madison Corpus of Early Spanish Manuscripts and Printings. Prepared by John ONeill, Madison and New York, 1999. CD-ROM ISBN 1-56954-122-1. Escorial Monasterio X-I-4

- *El emperador Otas de Roma*, Electronic Texts and Concordances of the Madison Corpus of Early Spanish Manuscripts and Printings. Prepared by John ONeill. (Madison and New York, 1999). CD-ROM. (ISBN 1-56954-122-1). Escorial: Monasterio h.I.13. Transcribed by Thomas D. Spaccarelli

- *Gran conquista de Ultramar*, Electronic Texts and Concordances of the Madison Corpus of Early Spanish Manuscripts and Printings. Prepared by John ONeill. (Madison and New York, 1999). CD-ROM. (ISBN 1-56954-122-1). Salamanca Giesser 1503-06-21.

- *Cuento de Tristán de Leonís*, Electronic Texts and Concordances of the Madison Corpus of Early Spanish Manuscripts and Printings. Prepared by John ONeill. (Madison and New York, 1999). CD-ROM. (ISBN 1-56954-122-1). Roma Vaticana 6428

- *Castigos e documentos de Sancho IV*, Electronic Texts and Concordances of the Madison Corpus of Early Spanish Manuscripts and Printings. Prepared by John ONeill. (Madison and New York, 1999). CD-ROM. (ISBN 1-56954-122-1). Madrid: Nacional MS. 6559. Transcribed by William Palmer & Craig Frazier (Directed by Frank Domínguez)

CP - Davies, Mark and Michael Ferreira. (2006-) *Corpus do Português: 45 million words, 1300s-1900s*. Available online at http://www.corpusdoportugues.org.

Hyperbase : logiciel documentaire et statistique pour l'exploration des textes. Recherche hypertextuelle dans la *Comédie Humaine* http://ancilla.unice.fr/

CICA - *Corpus Informatizat del Català Antic* (dirigit por Joan Torruella junt ab Manuel Pérez Saldanya i Josep Martines) http://www.cica.cat/.

CIPM - *Corpus Informatizado do Português Medieval*. Centro de Linguística da Universidade Nova de Lisboa - Faculdade de Ciências Sociais e Humanas sob a direcção de M. Francisca Xavier http://cipm.fcsh.unl.pt/

– *Demanda do Santo Graal*, in Nunes, Irene Freire (2001) *A Demanda do Santo Graal*. Versão revista e digitalizada com base na edição publicada pela Imprensa Nacional Casa da Moeda, Lisboa 1995, cedida pela editora.

– *Castelo Perigoso* (sem data), in Neto, João António Santana (ed.) (1997), *Duas Leituras do Tratado Ascético-Místico Castelo Perigoso*, Dissertação de Doutoramento, São Paulo, Faculdade de Filosofia, Letras e Ciências Humanas, USP. Edição revista por Irene Nunes e cedida pelo editor.

– *Crónica do Conde D. Pedro de Meneses* (sd), in Brocardo, Maria Teresa (ed.) (1994) *Crónica do Conde D. Pedro de Meneses*, Dissertação de Doutoramento, Lisboa, F.C.S.H., pp. 333–693. Edição digitalizada cedida pela editora.

– *7 Vidas de Santos de um Manuscrito Alcobacense* (cópias do século XV), in Castro, Ivo *et alii* (eds.) (1985) *Vidas de Santos de um Manuscrito Alcobacense* (Cod. Alc. cclxvi / antt 2274), Lisboa, INIC, pp. 16–52; 59–83.

– *Crónica de D. João I, parte 1*, in Lopes, Fernão (1945) *Crónica de D. João I*, Porto, Livraria Civilização Editora, vol. I (segundo o códice nº 352 do Arquivo Nacional da Torre do Tombo). Edição digitalizada cedida por José Barbosa Machado.

– *Crónica de D. João I, parte 2*, in Lopes, Fernão (1949) *Crónica de D. João Primeiro*, Porto, Livraria Civilização Editora. Edição digitalizada cedida por José Barbosa Machado.

LEX - Lexundria. *The Ten Books on Architecture*, translated by Joseph Gwilt http://lexundria.com/vitr/10.3/gw

LFA - Laboratoire de français ancien. Université d'Ottawa, Faculté des Arts. http://www.lfa.uottawa.ca/

Roman de Thèbes (anonyme). Éd. G. Raynaud de Lage, 2 tomes, Paris, Champion, 1966.

http://www.lfa.uottawa.ca/activites/textes/Thebes/thebespres.htm

Yvan Lepage, Transcription synoptique des manuscrits et fragments du *Couronnement de Louis*

http://www.lfa.uottawa.ca/activites/textes/Couronnement/coltexte.htm

TLFi. Trésor de la Langue Française informatisée. CNRTL – Centre National de Ressources Textuelles et Lexicales. Ortolang. http://www.cnrtl.fr/

Penelope. copyright © William P. Thayer. Marcus Vitruvius Pollio: de Architectura, Liber X.

http://penelope.uchicago.edu/Thayer/L/Roman/Texts/Vitruvius/10*.html

PER – Perseus Digital Library (Perseus 4.0 – Perseus Hopper), Gregory R. Crane, editor-in-chief – Tufts University.

Benef. L. Annaeus Seneca. Moral Essays: volume 3. John W. Basore. London and New York. Heinemann. 1935. http://data.perseus.org/citations/urn:cts:latinLit:phi1017.phi013.perseus-lat1:6.5.1

DECT - Dictionnaire Électronique de Chrétien de Troyes. Université d'Ottawa – ATILF : Analyse et Traitement Informatique de la Langue Française – CNRS – Université de Lorraine.

http://www.atilf.fr/dect

- Chrétien de Troyes. *Érec.* Pierre Kunstmann. Conseil de recherches en Sciences Humaines du Canada. manuscrit P (BnF fr. 794)
- Chrétien de Troyes. *Cligès.* Pierre Kunstmann. Conseil de recherches en Sciences Humaines du Canada. manuscrit P (BnF fr. 794)
- Chrétien de Troyes. *Lancelot ou Le Chevalier de la Charrette.* Pierre Kunstmann. Conseil de recherches en Sciences Humaines du Canada. manuscrit P (BnF fr. 794)
- Chrétien de Troyes. *Yvain ou Le Chevalier au Lion.* Pierre Kunstmann. Conseil de recherches en Sciences Humaines du Canada. manuscrit P (BnF fr. 794)
- Chrétien de Troyes. *Perceval.* Pierre Kunstmann. Conseil de recherches en Sciences Humaines du Canada. manuscrit P (BnF fr. 794)

HSMS. Gago Jover, Francisco (ed.). 2013. *Spanish Legal Texts. Digital Library of Old Spanish Texts.* Hispanic Seminary of Medieval Studies.

http://www.hispanicseminary/t&c/lex/index.htm

HTH - Quintus Curtius [*History of Alexander*] *with an English translation by John C. Rolfe.* Cambridge, Mass., Harvard Univ. Press, 1946

http://babel.hathitrust.org/cgi/pt?id=mdp.39015008158415;view=1up;seq=119

FGB - forgottenbooks

Centaurus, Chiro. (2013). pp. 198–9. *Claudii Hermeri Mulomedicina Chironis.* London: Forgotten Books. (Original work published 1901).

http://www.forgottenbooks.com/readbook_text/Claudii_Hermeri_Mulomedicina_Chironis_1500015716/237

Apuleius. (2013). pp. 138–9. *The Metamorphoses; Or Golden Ass: Translated By H. E. Butler* (Vol. 1). London: Forgotten Books. (Original work published 1910) http://www.forgottenbooks.com/readbook_text/The_Metamorphoses_Or_Golden_Ass_v1_1000643157/139

INTR - Titus Maccius Plautus. *Truculentus*. Printed source: T. Maccius Plautus. Plauti Comoediae. F. Leo. Berlin. Weidmann. 1895–1896 http://www.intra-text.com/IXT/LAT0549/_IDX019.HTM

LC – Loeb Classics

- Terence Volume I. Loeb Classical Library 22: *The Woman of Andros. The Self-Tormentor. The Eunuch*. Edited and translated by John Barsby. Publication: December 2001 DOI: 10.4159/DLCL.terence-woman_andros.2001

- Seneca Volume II. Loeb Classical Library 254: *Moral Essays, Volume II: De Consolatione ad Marciam. De Vita Beata. De Otio. De Tranquillitate Animi. De Brevitate Vitae. De Consolatione ad Polybium. De Consolatione ad Helviam*. Translated by John W. Basore. Publication: January 1932 DOI: 10.4159/DLCL.seneca_younger-de_vita_beata.1932

- Seneca Volume I. Loeb Classical Library 214: *Moral Essays, Volume I (De Providentia. De Constantia. De Ira. De Clementia)*. Translated by John W. Basore. Publication: January 1928. DOI: 10.4159/DLCL.seneca_younger-de_clementia.1928

- Cicero Volume XX. Loeb Classical Library 154: *On Old Age. On Friendship (Laelivs de Amicitia). On Divination*. Translated by W. A. Falconer. Publication: January 1923. DOI: 10.4159/DLCL.marcus_tullius_cicero-de_amicitia.1923

- Cicero Volume XIV. Loeb Classical Library 252: *Pro Milone. In Pisonem. Pro Scauro. Pro Fonteio (On Behalf of Fonteius). Pro Rabirio Postumo. Pro Marcello. Pro Ligario. Pro Rege Deiotaro*. Translated by N. H. Watts. Publication: January 1931 DOI: 10.4159/DLCL.marcus_tullius_cicero-pro_fonteio.1931

- Cicero Volume IX. Loeb Classical Library 198: *Pro Lege Manilia. Pro Caecina. Pro Cluentio. Pro Rabirio Perduellionis Reo*. Translated by H. Grose Hodge. Publication: January 1927. DOI: 10.4159/DLCL.marcus_tullius_cicero-pro_cluentio.1927

PG - Project Gutenberg's

- Off. Marcus Tullius Cicero, *De Officiis*. Translator: Walter Miller (Release Date: September 29, 2014). Produced by Ted Garvin and the Online Distributed Proofreading Team

- https://www.gutenberg.org/files/47001/47001-h/47001-h.htm

- Ora. Marcus Tullius Cicero, *The Orator of M.T. Cicero. Addressed to Marcus Brutus. (The Orations of Marcus Tullius Cicero, Volume 4)*. (Release Date: February 14, 2004). Produced by Ted Garvin and PG Distributed Proofreaders
  http://www.gutenberg.org/cache/epub/11080/pg11080-images.html

- Nat. Marcus Tullius Cicero, *Tusculan Disputations* (also, *Treatises On The Nature Of The Gods, And On The Commonwealth*) (Release Date: February 9, 2005). Produced by Ted Garvin, Hagen von Eitzen and the PG Online Distributed Proofreading Team.
  https://www.gutenberg.org/files/14988/14988-h/14988-h.htm

- Tusc. Marcus Tullius Cicero, *Tusculan Disputations* (also, *Treatises On The Nature Of The Gods, And On The Commonwealth*) (Release Date: February 9, 2005). Produced by Ted Garvin, Hagen von Eitzen and the PG Online Distributed Proofreading Team.
  https://www.gutenberg.org/files/14988/14988-h/14988-h.htm

- Caius Julius Caesar, *De Bello Gallico and Other Commentaries* (Release Date: January 9, 2004). Produced by Stan Goodman, Ted Garvin, Carol David and PG Distributed Proofreaders
  http://www.gutenberg.org/cache/epub/10657/pg10657-images.html

- François Rabelais, *Gargantua and Pantagruel. Five Books Of The Lives, Heroic Deeds And Sayings Of Gargantua And His Son Pantagruel.* (Release Date: August 8, 2004). Produced by Sue Asscher and David Widger
  http://www.gutenberg.org/files/1200/1200-h/1200-h.htm#link22HCH0014)

- Sallust, *Conspiracy of Catiline and The Jurgurthine War* (Release Date: April, 2005 First Posted: June 10, 2003). Produced by David Starner, Marc D'Hooghe, Charles Franks and the Online Distributed Proofreading Team.
  http://www.gutenberg.org/cache/epub/7990/pg7990.html

- Seneca, *L. Annaeus Seneca On Benefits.* Editor: Aubrey Stewart (Release Date: December 3, 2009). Produced by Charles Franks, Robert Rowe, David Widger, and the Online Distributed Proofreading Team. http://www.gutenberg.org/files/3794/3794-h/3794-h.htm

- Titus Livius, *The History of Rome*, Books 01 to 08 (Release Date: November 6, 2006). Produced by Ted Garvin, Taavi Kalju and the Online Distributed Proofreading Team at
  http://www.gutenberg.org/files/19725/19725-h/19725-h.htm

- Titus Livius, *The History of Rome*, Books Nine to Twenty-Six (Release Date: February 1, 2004). E-text prepared by Ted Garvin, Ben Courtney, and Project Gutenberg Distributed Proofreaders
  http://www.gutenberg.org/files/10907/10907-h/10907-h.htm

- Titus Livius, *History of Rome, Vol III* (Release Date: June 11, 2004). Produced by Ted Garvin, Bill Hershey and PG Distributed Proofreaders

  http://www.gutenberg.org/files/12582/12582-h/12582-h.htm
- Virgil, *The Aeneid of Virgil*. Translated into English Verse by E. Fairfax Taylor. Editor: Ernest Rhys. Commentator: Maine J. P. (Release Date: May 28, 2006). Produced by Ron Swanson

  http://www.gutenberg.org/files/18466/18466-h/18466-h.htm
- Virgil, *The Aeneid of Virgil*. Translated by J. W. Mackail (Release Date: August 29, 2007). E-text prepared by David Clarke, Lisa Reigel, and the Project Gutenberg Online Distributed Proofreading Team

  http://www.gutenberg.org/files/22456/22456-h/22456-h.htm

ST - *The Works of Tacitus*, tr. by Alfred John Church and William Jackson Brodribb [1864–1877]

http://www.sacred-texts.com/cla/tac/ag01000.htm

Scuola - *Giustino Historiarum Philippicarum T Pompeii Trogi Libri* XLIV, Liber XI 9

http://www.scuolazoo.com/appunti/versioni-latino/giustino/historiarum-philippicarum-t-pompeii-trogi-libri-xliv-33931/liber-xi-33931/versione/interea-darius-cum-cccc-milibus-peditum-ac-centum-milibus/

Tertullian – Justin, Epitome of Pompeius Trogus (1886). pp. 90–171 Books 11–20, transcribed by Roger Pearse, Ipswich, UK, 2003 http://www.tertullian.org/fathers/justinus_04_books11to20.htm

TLL – The Latin Library.
- *C. Ivli Caesaris Commentariorvm de Bello Gallico Liber Qvintvs*. Books V-VIII posted by William D. Carey and William L. Carey from the Loeb edition of 1919. The text is that of Nipperdey (1847) and R. du Pontet with corrections from T. Rice Holmes (1914).

  http://www.thelatinlibrary.com/caesar/gall5.shtml
- *C. Ivli Caesaris Commentariorvm de Bello Gallico Liber Sextvs*. Books V-VIII posted by William D. Carey and William L. Carey from the Loeb edition of 1919. The text is that of Nipperdey (1847) and R. du Pontet with corrections from T. Rice Holmes (1914).

  http://www.thelatinlibrary.com/caesar/gall6.shtml
- *C. Ivli Caesaris Commentariorvm de Bello Gallico Liber Secvndvs*. Books I-IV posted by Konrad Schroder from T. Rice Holmes, *C. Iuli Caesaris Commentarii Rerum in Gallia Gestarum VII A. Hirti Commentarius VIII* (Oxford University Press, 1914)

  http://www.thelatinlibrary.com/caesar/gall2.shtml

- *C. Ivli Caesaris Commentariorvm de Bello Gallico Liber Tertivs.* Books I-IV posted by Konrad Schroder from T. Rice Holmes, *C. Iuli Caesaris Commentarii Rerum in Gallia Gestarum VII A. Hirti Commentarius VIII* (Oxford University Press, 1914)

  http://www.thelatinlibrary.com/caesar/gall3.shtml
- *Apvlei Metamorphoseon Liber V* (no further data)

  http://www.thelatinlibrary.com/apuleius/apuleius5.shtml
- *M. Tvlli Ciceronis Tvscvlanarvm Dispvtationvm Liber Primvs*, submitted by Tomokazu Hanafusa, Japan. http://www.thelatinlibrary.com/cicero/tusc1.shtml
- *M. Tvlli Ciceronis De Navra Deorvm ad M. Brvtvm Liber Secvndvs* submitted by Erich Schweizer-Ferrari in Luzern, Switzerland. The text is that of W. Ax (post O. Plasberg), 2nd ed., Stuttgart 1933 (Teubner). http://www.thelatinlibrary.com/cicero/nd2.shtml
- *M. Tvlii Ciceronis Orator ad M. Brvtvm* (no further data)

  http://www.thelatinlibrary.com/cicero/orator.shtml
- *C. Sallvsti Crispi Bellvm Ivgurthinvm* (no further data)

  http://www.thelatinlibrary.com/sall.2.html
- Curtius Rufus, *Historiae Alexandri Magni Liber Tertius*, submitted by Juan José Marcos (Plasencia, Spain). http://www.thelatinlibrary.com/curtius/curtius3.shtml
- *P. Vergili Maronis Aeneidos Liber Septimvs* posted by Konrad Schroder from J. B. Greenough, *Bucolics, Aeneid, and Georgics of Vergil* (Boston: Ginn & Co., 1900) http://www.thelatinlibrary.com/vergil/aen7.shtml
- *P. Vergili Maronis Aeneidos Liber Decimvs* posted by Konrad Schroder from J. B. Greenough, *Bucolics, Aeneid, and Georgics of Vergil* (Boston: Ginn & Co., 1900)

  http://www.thelatinlibrary.com/vergil/aen10.shtml
- *Titi Livi Ab vrbe condita Liber V* posted by William Carey from the Walters-Conway edition of 1919. http://www.thelatinlibrary.com/cred.html
- *Titi Livi Ab vrbe condita Liber VIII* posted by William Carey from the Walters-Conway edition of 1919 and the B.O. Foster edition of 1924. http://www.thelatinlibrary.com/livy/liv.8.shtml
- *Titi Livi Ab vrbe condita Liber IX* (no further data) http://www.thelatinlibrary.com/livy/liv.9.shtml
- *Titi Livi Ab vrbe condita Liber X* (no further data) http://www.thelatinlibrary.com/livy/liv.10.shtml

- *Titi Livi Ab vrbe condita Liber XXI*, posted by William Carey from a compilation of texts, primarily the Loeb edition of B.O. Foster (1929), in turn based chiefly on the edition of August Luchs (Berlin 1888) and the Weissenborn-Müller edition of 1905. http://www.thelatinlibrary.com/livy/liv.21.shtml
- *Titi Livi Ab vrbe condita Liber XXVI* (no further data) http://www.thelatinlibrary.com/livy/liv.26.shtml
- *Titi Livi Ab vrbe condita Liber XXXIII* (no further data) http://www.thelatinlibrary.com/livy/liv.33.shtml

Index of Names

ŁÓDŹ
Studies in Language

Edited by
Barbara Lewandowska-Tomaszczyk and Łukasz Bogucki

www.peterlang.com